The Empress Theodora

T0327115

The Empress Theodora

Partner of Justinian

J A M E S   A L L A N   E V A N S

 University of Texas Press, Austin

This book has been supported by an endowment dedicated
to classics and the ancient world, funded by grants from the
National Endowment for the Humanities, the Gladys Krieble
Delmas Foundation, the James R. Dougherty, Jr. Foundation,
and the Rachael and Ben Vaughan Foundation, and by gifts
from Mark and Jo Ann Finley, Lucy Shoe Meritt, Anne Byrd
Nalle, and other individual donors.

Copyright © 2002 by the University of Texas Press
All rights reserved
Printed in the United States of America
First edition, 2002

Requests for permission to reproduce material from this work
should be sent to Permissions, University of Texas Press,
P.O. Box 7819, Austin, TX 78713-7819.

⊗ The paper used in this book meets the minimum
requirements of ANSI/NISO Z39.48-1992 (R1997)
(Permanence of Paper).

LIBRARY OF CONGRESS
CATALOGING-IN-PUBLICATION DATA

Evans, J. A. S. (James Allan Stewart), date
The empress Theodora : partner of Justinian / James Allan
Evans.— 1st ed.
    p.   cm.
Includes bibliographical references and index.
ISBN 978-0-292-70270-7

1. Theodora, Empress, consort of Justinian I, Emperor of the
East, d. 548   2. Byzantine Empire—History—Justinian I,
527-565.   3. Empresses—Byzantine Empire—Biography.
I. Title.
DF572.5 .E83   2002
949.5′013′092—dc21

                                        2001008471

Contents

Preface

This is a study that grew out of my earlier book on the Justinianic period, *The Age of Justinian: The Circumstances of Imperial Power*, published in 1996, and it, in turn, emerged from an interest in Procopius of Caesarea, whose contribution to tabloid-style journalism, popularly known as the *Secret History*, has permanently colored Theodora's reputation. The conviction grew on me that the empress Theodora deserved a book of her own. Not that she has failed to attract attention in the past. Cardinal Baronius, writing before Procopius' *Secret History* was discovered in the Vatican Library, thought she played Delilah to Justinian's Samson. Edward Gibbon, who had the *Secret History* to inform his views, hailed her as the "famous Theodora, whose strange elevation cannot be applauded as a triumph of human virtue." But she has had defenders. Charles Diehl wrote a gallant biography of her almost one hundred years ago, and it is still a valuable study, but he did not allow footnotes to impede his romantic impulses.[1] The best of the more recent books is Anthony Bridge's *Theodora: Portrait in a Byzantine Landscape*,[2] but, like Diehl's biography, it does not cite sources. Footnotes in a book intended to appeal to the general reading public should never overwhelm, but they are a reassuring presence.

There are a number of people whom I want to thank for their encouragement and help: the late Robert Browning whose correspondence was always reassuring, Geoffrey Greatrex of Dalhousie University who kept a constant flow of offprints coming my way, Jim Burr of the University of Texas Press, Wendy Waters, whose help with the maps was invaluable, and, by no means least, my wife, Eleanor, who patiently endured a woolgathering spouse. But in particular I want to thank the American School of Classical Studies in Athens, where I spent a productive year as a Whitehead Visiting Professor after I had retired from the University of British Columbia and offered a seminar on Late Antiquity to one of the best groups of graduate students I have taught. It was a stimulating experience for me, and it is to them that I dedicate this book.

Introduction

Our knowledge of the past is as good as our sources, and that is true of no one more than the empress Theodora. She still looks down at us from the chancel wall of San Vitale in Ravenna: a small woman with an oval face and arresting eyes. Even if we knew nothing about her, her portrait would still be riveting. But, in fact, Theodora is a character from the past who left a mark on history sufficiently indelible that writers, both contemporary and retrospective, took note. Empresses before Theodora had wielded influence and even dominated the court, particularly when weak emperors such as Arcadius and Theodosius II were on the throne, but none had been the acknowledged partner of her husband. Theodora was, to quote Justinian's own words in one of his laws, "our most pious consort given us by God."

Our most important source, the one that most colors our perception of Theodora, is Procopius of Caesarea.[1] He was a member of the general staff of Belisarius, the field marshal who is the best known of all Justinian's officers thanks to the writings of Procopius. He produced a history of Justinian's wars that must have been more or less complete by 545, but before he released it to the small reading public in Constantinople that could appreciate his Attic prose, he continued it to include events up to the middle of the century. The latest can be dated to 551.[2] There he stopped, even though 551 was not a natural stopping place, for the wars Justinian waged continued, and at midcentury Procopius could not see the end of them.

The work falls into three sections: the first two books relate the war against Persia, books three and four the war in Africa, dealing first with the overthrow of the Vandal kingdom and then the pacification of Africa, and books five to seven the war against the Ostrogoths in Italy. Procopius wrote self-consciously in the tradition of the great classical historians, Herodotus and Thucydides, and it was possibly from Appian that he borrowed his plan of dividing the war into three fronts and dealing with them separately. The focus of the *History of the Wars* is not Theodora, or even Justinian himself; yet Theodora periodically makes an entrance. It is from the *Wars* that we have the magnificent description of how Theodora rallied the government when it seemed as if the Nika revolt would force it to flee, and for better or worse, this description has colored the perception of later historians. It is the basis for the romantic concept of Theodora as heroine: a woman with the masculine virtue of coolness under fire while the men around her panicked. But the speech with which Theodora rallied Justinian's court is a rhetorical composition, and whether or not Theodora actually spoke it or anything like it is a matter of opinion.

Procopius added an eighth book to the *Wars*, but it covers the years after Theodora's death, from where the first seven books break off until the final victory in Italy in 552. He wrote another work for publication as well, a panegyric that describes Justinian's building program. It is an uneven work; the first book deals with Constantinople and the buildings Justinian constructed there, and since it ignores the collapse in 558 of the first dome of Hagia Sophia, the greatest church built by Justinian, we must believe either that it was written earlier or that Procopius had a remarkable ability to turn a blind eye to events that did not contribute to his hagiography. Internal evidence suggests that the last five books were written two or three years later. Theodora, in any event, was dead by the time *On the Buildings* was composed, and we learn nothing of her role as builder from it, though there is a flattering reference to her beauty.[3] The focus of the panegyric is Justinian and his care for his subjects. Procopius omits Theodora's share in it.

A reference in the late-tenth-century Byzantine lexicon known as the *Souda* alerted scholars to another composition of Procopius, the *Anekdota*, or *Unpublished Works*, but it was known only from the *Souda*'s description until the Vatican librarian Niccolò Alemmani found a copy in his library and published it in 1623. The *Souda* refers to it as a *komodia*, a comic burlesque, and it is a satire intended to arouse peevish sniggers, but the humor is as bitter as anything Juvenal ever wrote. The *Secret History*, as the composition came to be known, was a slashing attack. It compares Justinian's regime with the epidemic of bubonic plague in 542 to the plague's advantage, for half the population survived the plague, but no one escaped the emperor's rapacity.[4]

Its particular targets are Belisarius, his wife, Antonina, Justinian, and Theodora. The *Secret History* revealed that Theodora's father had been a bear keeper in the Hippodrome and that she had been a burlesque queen.

In Late Antiquity, women in the theater were considered no better than harlots, though even among them there were upper and lower classes: the lower class consisted of the women who danced and cavorted in the theater orchestras, and a cut above them were those who performed mimes on the stage. The former practiced common prostitution as a sideline. Antonina's mother had belonged to this group. The latter were courtesans, serving customers of a better class, but they still sold sexual favors, and Theodora was one of their number. She made no secret of it; after she became empress, old female friends from the theater were welcome in the palace. Inevitably salacious stories circulated about her life in the theater, and Procopius retails them gleefully.

The *Secret History* is a hostile source written by an embitterered man. It would be hard to say whether Procopius' animus against Theodora and Antonina was based more on male chauvinism directed against women in power or on contempt for their origins: at one point the *Secret History* indicates with venom that Justinian could have had his choice of upper-class women for a wife, and instead he chose a slut from the very dregs of society. Both prejudices were at work, but one feels that if Theodora had come to the throne with the social standing of a woman like Anicia Juliana, who built the church of Saint Polyeuktos in Constantinople in the 520s and whose impeccable connections included the emperor Valentinian III as grandfather and a niece of the old emperor Anastasius as daughter-in-law,[5] Procopius' male chauvinism would have faded noticeably.

Yet clearly a good deal of what the *Secret History* reports is not fiction. The *Ecclesiastical History* of Evagrius Scholasticus, a lawyer of Antioch whose history ends with the year 594, repeats the surmise of the *Secret History* that Theodora and Justinian only pretended to oppose each other on the burning theological question of the day, the rift between the Monophysites and the Chalcedonians over the nature of Christ. It is unlikely that Evagrius found a copy of the *Secret History* to read. Rather both authors were reporting a notion that was widely held among the Chalcedonians, who distrusted Theodora and grouped her with their enemies. The Monophysites, on the other hand, considered her a refuge in time of need. Yet the protection she gave the persecuted Monophysite monks and clergy was double-edged. She turned the Palace of Hormisdas into a monastery for them, thus protecting them from Chalcedonian fury. But by so doing, she kept them isolated. Justin I's persecution had made martyrs out of the Monophysites. Monks and holy men were forced out of their monasteries and sought refuge in the villages, where they mingled with the laity and spread their doctrines. The Palace of Hormisdas was both a safe house and a quarantine.

As time went on, particularly after the plague that began in 541 in Egypt and Syria and smote Constantinople the next year, Theodora seems to have acted with greater independence: it was in the 540s that she made the momentous move that led to the establishment of separate Monophysite churches in the eastern provinces and Egypt.[6] But for all that, Theodora and Justinian remained collaborators. The fact is that although Rome regarded Monophysitism as a heresy, neither Justinian nor Theodora did. For them the problem was simply a division between two differing theological interpretations, and reasonable persons should be able to bridge it.

John of Ephesus, whose connection with Ephesus was tenuous (he was ordained bishop of Ephesus by Jacob Bara'dai, the titular Monophysite bishop of Edessa, modern Urfa, in 558), was born in a village near Amida, nowadays Diyarbakir, about 507 and at age three or four became an oblate in the nearby monastery of the stylite saint Maro whose ministrations had saved his life when he was an infant. At Maro's death John was fifteen, and he moved to a monastery at Amida where the monks were Monophysite. The persecution unleashed in 521 by Justin I at the direction of Pope Hormisdas drove the monks from their monastery, and they were not allowed to return until the persecution paused in 530, a respite for which they could thank Theodora. John, however, was no longer interested in the contemplative life. He traveled from monastery to monastery, visiting Egypt in 534 and Constantinople in 535. He knew and liked Theodora, and in 542 Justinian selected him to convert the remaining pagans in Asia Minor, on condition that he convert them to the Chalcedonian faith. Probably, however, he did not conceal his own Monophysite beliefs, for when Jacob Bara'dai passed through the area, he consecrated seven bishops there. John's own bishopric was nominally Ephesus, which was the metropolis of Asia, and hence John's alternate sobriquet is John of Asia. He spent no time in Ephesus. His native tongue was Syriac, but he was at home in Greek.

John wrote an ecclesiastical history in three parts, of which the third survives in a manuscript found in the mid-nineteenth century at the desert monastery of Saint Mary Deipara in Egypt. It covers the years 571–86. The second section, which probably started with the emperor Theodosius II, partially survives at second hand in the the *Chronicle of Zuqnin*, also known as the *Chronicle of Pseudo-Dionysius of Tel-Mahre,* in the *Chronicle* of Michael the Syrian, and in the *Chronography* of Elias Bar Shinaya (975-1049), a Nestorian priest who became the metropolitan bishop of Nisibis in Mesopotamia and wrote his chronicle in Syriac, which survives in one mutilated manuscript in the British Library. The universal *Chronicle* once attributed to Dionysius of Tel-Mahre was written at the end of the eighth century by an unknown author at the monastery of Zuqnin in northern Mesopotamia. From it we have a verbatim quotation of John's long, vivid description of the plague that struck the empire in 541-42. As for Michael the Syrian, who was a well-educated monk elected Jacobite patriarch of Antioch in 1166, his universal *Chronicle* is the longest and most ambitious Syriac chronicle that we have. It survives in one privately owned manuscript in Urfa.[7] These are muddled sources, but they preserve Syriac tradition and give us occasional glimpses of Theodora.

It is John's *Lives of the Eastern Saints*[8] that best furnishes impressions of Theodora as seen by Monophysite eyes. This tract recounts the lives of fifty-eight holy men and women. Occasionally Theodora intrudes in the stories. It is from John's report of Stephen, deacon to Mare, bishop of Amida, that we have a reference to Theodora "who came from the brothel." The words are in Greek in the midst of John's Syriac text, which may indicate that they are a later insertion, but probably not. It is more likely that John is reproducing a popular epithet he heard on the streets of Constantinople, where the details of Theodora's early life were common knowledge. He repeated it without malice. In John's writings there is no hint of the prurience that we sense in Procopius' *Secret History.* But the reference corroborates at least some of the malicious gossip that the *Secret History* reports.

The Syriac sources are friendly, but even so, the essential toughness of the empress is not concealed. The Syriac chronicle of Zachariah of Mytilene[9] reports Theodora's insistence that the nephews of the old emperor Anastasius, Hypatius and Pompeius, be executed after the Nika riots. Justinian was more inclined to mercy. The Latin and Greek sources, when they are not hostile, tend to be either neutral or brief. John the Lydian, who hated the praetorian prefect John the Cappadocian, should have been an admirer, but he makes only one mention of her in his *On the Magistracies.*[10] Justinian, said John, had failed to notice John's many iniquities, and his courtiers were afraid to speak out, but Theodora realized that John was ruining the state and warned her husband. Theodora, we are told, was vigilant and particularly sympathetic toward those who suffered wrong. The Lydian's portrayal of Theodora reflects the public persona she cultivated. In fact, it was her own authority that she was vigilant to protect, and, recognizing John the Cappadocian as a threat, she baited a trap for him and brought him down. Even after he was humbled she continued to pursue him. Theodora did not forgive easily.

We get another brief glimpse of Theodora exercising ruthless power in the *Book of the Popes* (Liber Pontificalis), a series of brief papal biographies from Saint Peter to the late ninth century. Similarly, in the *Variae* of Cassiodorus Senator, 468 ornate letters, *formulae* (model letters), and edicts that Cassiodorus produced in the service of the Ostrogothic rulers of Italy, we get a fleeting impression of Theodora carrying on an obscure negotiation with the Ostrogothic king Theodahad and his queen, Gudeliva. It gives some substance to the charge in the *Secret History* that Theodora arranged the murder of Theodoric the Ostrogoth's daughter, Amalasuintha, but the language is cryptic. The charge remains unproved. But the letter gives a glimpse of the double-pronged diplomacy of Justinian and Theodora, which proceeded on two levels, the official level of the emperor and the covert, slightly underhand level of the empress.

Eusebius of Caesarea in the fourth century set the fashion for world chronicles, and they acquired great popularity in Late Antiquity.[11] They were written in Greek, Latin, and, as we have seen, Syriac. We have the world chronicle of John Malalas, the *Chronicon Paschale*, the chronicle of Theophanes Confessor, and that of Victor, bishop of Tonnena in Africa, who supplies our only report of how Theodora died, to name only those that are most important for our subject. The name Malalas comes from *malal*, the Syriac word for *rhetor*, so that we may infer that John Malalas was a lawyer. He was educated in Antioch and probably was a civil servant there, but at some point early in Justinian's reign, he moved to Constantinople. Perhaps for that reason, the eighteenth book dealing with Justinian's reign seems well acquainted with official propaganda and is colored by it. The *Chronicon Paschale*, or *Easter Chronicle*, so called because of its unknown author's interest in determining the date of Easter, belongs to the seventh century, and Theophanes (ca. 760–817) wrote a *Chronographia* that is as good as its sources. Unfortunately we are not always certain what those sources were. Procopius and Malalas, certainly, for Justinian's reign. Perhaps others.

Procopius dominates. The *Secret History* colors our assessment of Theodora. It tells how she rose from the theater to the throne and how she used the power she acquired. Her acumen was respected by Justinian, whose law code was one of the greatest legacies of the ancient world to its modern counterpart. Yet the *Secret History* is clear evidence of the bitter, visceral hatred she could inspire. Malicious gossip is a weapon of the disempowered, and to the social strata to which Procopius either belonged or wanted to belong, Theodora represented the threat of social revolution. Her lower-class origins, which she flaunted—she brought old friends from the theater into the palace—gave offense, but even more offensive was her insistence on receiving obeisance. Her emphasis on court ceremonial was punctilious. She took delight in seeing members of the old elite groveling before her. Justinian was not much better; his was a family of Thracian peasants brought into high society by the emperor Justin whom luck mingled with cunning had brought unexpectedly to the throne. Together Justinian and Theodora represented change in a society that distrusted innovation. Theodora was a parvenue in a culture where status mattered, self-educated in circles where schooling in the Greek classics was the mark of breeding, and a Monophysite in a court where orthodoxy was defined by the Chalcedonian Creed. The great French Byzantinist Charles Diehl[12] romanticized her; Sarah Bernhardt depicted her on stage in a play by Victorien Sardou that improved upon history: the stage Theodora had a lover and was strangled on Justinian's orders, a far more romantic end than the bare bones of history supplies. Theodora, to quote Robert Browning, "remains an enigmatic and rather alarming figure, a woman enjoying immense power in an age which had no institutional structure for such exercise of power. Later tradition tended to close its eyes to her."[13]

I began writing this book in 1998–99, while I was a Whitehead Visiting Professor at the American School of Classical Studies in Athens, where I could use the resources of the Gennadius Library and of the British School of Archaeology. But the idea came to me earlier, in 1997, while I was a visiting professor of history at the University of Washington. My *Age of Justinian* had just appeared, but it seemed to me that Theodora played a peculiar role in Justinian's age as both supporter and opponent of the emperor, and it deserved examination. Was the regime of Theodora and Justinian a dyarchy in which the emperor and the empress promoted divergent policies? Was it true that they had two different visions of statecraft, Justinian dazzled by a longing to restore the ancient Roman Empire and Theodora convinced that the empire's heart belonged to the east, and its strength lay in the provinces of the Orient? What kept these two very different strong-willed persons in partnership?[14] Conjugal affection is somewhat out of style as an explanation, and sexual attraction (Procopius suspected animal lust) is time-sensitive: it rarely lasts forever. Yet the partnership of Justinian and Theodora remained firm even after Theodora's death. The imperial team complemented each other, even in their differences, and both were utterly loyal. Perhaps the glue of the partnership was mutual respect.

Finally, what did Theodora accomplish? Perhaps her one lasting achievement was an inadvertent one: she helped to make the rift between Monophysite and Chalcedonian permanent. But whether the rift would have been bridged without her interventions is a question that belongs to the special genre of "Might-Have-Been History," and that is not history at all.

View of the church of Hagia Sophia, built by Justinian and Theodora after the previous basilica church of Hagia Sophia was destroyed in the Nika riots, 532. *Courtesy of the Embassy of Turkey, Ottawa*

View of the interior of Hagia Sophia. *Courtesy of the Embassy of Turkey, Ottawa*

A general view of Hagia Sophia, now a museum in modern Istanbul. *Photo by James Allan Evans*

The deserted monastery at Alahan above the Göksu River Gorge in Turkey. Built under the reign of the emperor Zeno, the monastery was probably Monophysite and was deserted at the time of the Monophysite persecution initiated by Justin I. It was reinhabited later at an unknown date. *Photo by James Allan Evans*

The interior of the East Church at the monastery of Alahan.
Photo by James Allan Evans

The Theodosian Walls of Constantinople and the Charisius Gate, through which the road from Singidunum (modern Belgrade) entered the city. *Photo by James Allan Evans*

View of the church of Saints Sergius and Bacchus in Istanbul. Now Küçuk Aya Sofya Camii. *Photo by James Allan Evans*

Mosaic from the chancel of San Vitale in Ravenna, dedicated in 547. Theodora dominates the center of the composition, and the two women on her left have tentatively been identified as Antonina, the wife of Belisarius, and their daughter, Joannina. The mosaic may be based on a picture commemorating the betrothal of Joannina and the grandson of Theodora. *Courtesy of Alinari/Art Resource*

View of the church of Saints Sergius and Bacchus. Built near the Hormisdas Palace at the start of Justinian and Theodora's reign, it may have been the church used by the Monophysite refugees whom Theodora supported in the Hormisdas Palace. *Courtesy of Dumbarton Oaks, Washington, D.C.*

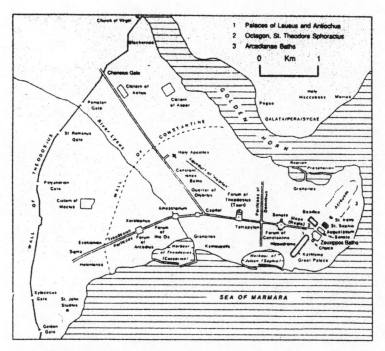

MAP 1. Constantinople

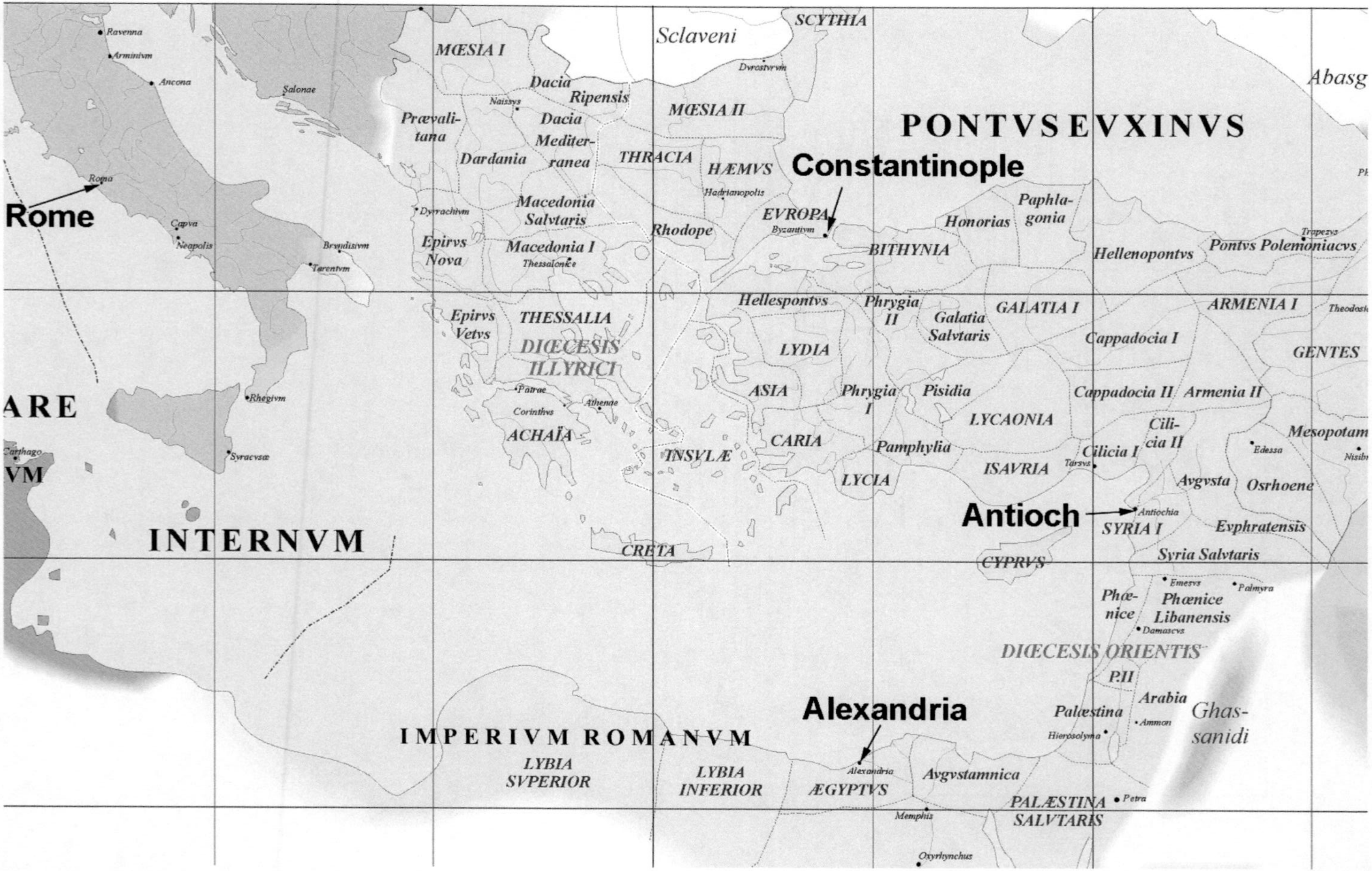

MAP 2. The Four Cities (courtesy Christos Nüssli)

The Empress Theodora

A New Dynasty Takes Power

The Old Order Changes: The Death of Anastasius

The Constantinople of the opening decades of the sixth century, which the empress Theodora knew as a child, was a cosmopolitan city where wealth and poverty rubbed shoulders and palaces, workshops, monasteries, and churches crowded the streets. She was familiar with its core, for there her family lived, where the imperial palace sprawled over the southeast tip of the city, with the great Hippodrome beside it; beyond, the Baths of Zeuxippos that opened on to the city's main street, the Mese, and to the east, the square called the Augustaeum that fronted the patriarchal church of Hagia Sophia. Since the emperor Constantine founded Constantinople in 330 as the capital of a Christian empire, it had grown to some half million souls. Although bubonic plague cut deeply into the city's population in 542, until then it continued to expand, fed by an influx of provincials seeking a better life: their numbers were so great that a special officer called a *quaesitor* was established to regulate the migration.[1] When the emperor Anastasius died in 518, he left a full treasury: Procopius[2] reports that it held a surplus of 320,000 gold pounds. That is a very large amount, huge by the standards of the day, and we may suspect some exaggeration, for Procopius was making a pointed contrast with this statistic between the prudence of the good old emperor Anastasius and the profligacy of his successors, Justin and Justinian, who rapidly wasted the surplus. Yet even if Procopius was guilty of exaggeration, we need not doubt that Anastasius left the imperial treasury abundantly full, for his was a prosperous reign, and he had managed to avoid any major disaster.

On the eastern frontier, there had been a war with Persia from 502 to 506, in the course of which Anastasius updated the defenses of the cities and border strongholds that were vulnerable to Persian invasion.[3] On the fringe of the empire within a few miles of Nisibis, which the Roman Empire had been compelled to surrender after the collapse of the emperor Julian's expedition against Persia two and a half centuries earlier, he built the great fortress of Dara. Its construction contravened a treaty of 442, as the Persians were not infrequently to point out, but the Persian king Kavadh was in no position to do more than protest, and in 506 he agreed to a truce that gave the East two decades of peace. On the Danube and the Black Sea coast where the Hun invasions of the mid-fifth century had shattered the settlements, forts were rebuilt and cities repeopled, and although a succession of raiders in the sixth century would pierce the frontier and pillage the prefecture of Illyricum, there would be no permanent Slavic settlements south of the Danube until the end of the century.[4]

It was very different in the west, where the emperors were long gone. Odacer, a warlord who headed a mixed group of barbarians, had packed the last emperor, a boy named Romulus Augustulus, off into retirement in 476. The imperial palace on the Palatine Hill in Rome stood empty, and in Ravenna, where the last emperors in the west had taken refuge, there ruled an Ostrogothic king, Theodoric the Amal, who had defeated and then murdered Odacer. Theodoric had invaded Italy with the blessing of Anastasius' predecessor, Zeno, who found him an unruly neighbor in the Balkans and encouraged the Italian invasion as a way of getting rid of him. Anastasius had regularized Theodoric's position in 498, recognizing him as *rex*. The title *rex* was now reserved for barbarian kings, and it was as a barbarian king that Theodoric ruled his Ostrogoths, but the Romans still owed their loyalty to their emperor even though the real power in Italy lay with Theodoric. The mentality of Late Antiquity recognized no decline and fall of the empire. The people considered themselves Romans whatever their native tongues might be, and once the imperial throne in the west was empty, this empire of the mind looked to the one remaining emperor, whose capital was Constantinople.

Anastasius came from a distinguished family, but he had no son, though there were three nephews, Probus, Pompeius, and Hypatius. The eldest, Hypatius, was an experienced soldier, but as a military commander he was thoroughly mediocre and during his whole career never won a victory or even took part in a successful military operation.[5] Yet if Anastasius' death had not been quite as unexpected and if Hypatius had been at his bedside when he died during the night of 8–9 July, the throne would probably have passed smoothly into his hands. But on that night Hypatius was not in Constantinople. He was in Antioch, the headquarters of the Master of Soldiers in the East, which office he held. The field was open.

Anastasius himself had been the choice of the Augusta Ariadne,[6] widow of the emperor Zeno, who was herself the daughter of Leo I, and she reinforced Anastasius' legitimacy by marrying him a month after his accession. But in 518 there was no empress still alive to take charge and no clear procedure for choosing Anastasius' successor, though legal tradition gave the senate the right to choose and the people the right to ratify the choice. Thus the Grand Chamberlain and his company of thirty court ushers, known as the Silentiaries, reported the emperor's death to the Master of Offices, Celer, the commander of the palatine guardsmen known as the Scholarians, who were more ornamental than effective, and to Justin, the Count of the Excubitors, who, unlike the Scholarians, were effective troops and could fight if required. Both officers summoned their men. Morning came. The people assembled in the Hippodrome and waited there expectantly, while within the Great Palace the senate gathered and met with the important imperial officials and the patriarch in the Hall of the Nineteen Couches to choose the next emperor. Celer, who wanted a smooth transition—he was suffering from gout, which cannot have improved his patience with lengthy contention—urged the senate to act quickly and make a choice. But the negotiations were difficult, and the haggling dragged on while the people in the Hippodrome grew impatient. Meanwhile the Excubitors put forward a candidate, but he would not do. Then the Scholarians presented a candidate, but the Excubitors manhandled him, and he might have been killed if Justin's nephew, Justinian, had not intervened. The story goes that then the Scholarians suggested Justinian himself, but that is hard to believe. Justinian was still a young guardsman with no following. Finally the senate, which was by now a little frightened, elected Justin. He was crowned forthwith in the *kathisma,* the imperial loge in the Hippodrome, and the people acclaimed him "Augustus" and his wife "Augusta."

Justin was a compromise candidate without powerful enemies, and his old age was no disadvantage. He cannot have been expected to live long. Procopius,[7] who despised him, claimed that he was an illiterate old man, as stupid as a donkey. No one, least of all himself, expected him to initiate the most brilliant epoch of the proto-Byzantine period. But there were reports of skullduggery behind the scenes, which show that he was anything but a simple fool. He secured his election as emperor by a double cross. The Grand Chamberlain, Amantius, coveted power, and since he was a eunuch and thus could not himself become emperor, he schemed to put one of his domestics, Theocritus, on the throne. Amantius entrusted Justin with money to make the necessary bribes. But Justin distributed the money on his own behalf, and to the chagrin of the Grand Chamberlain, the next emperor was Justin himself.[8]

Justin moved with speed and ruthless determination to consolidate his power. Not ten days after his coronation, he executed Amantius, charging him with insulting the patriarch. Three other chamberlains who were part of Amantius' cabal were arrested; two were executed and one exiled, and as for Theocritus himself, he was seized, killed in prison, and his body thrown into the sea.[9] John the Lydian was to remark that Anastasius' able but unpopular praetorian prefect, Marinus, and all who had owed their advancement to the old emperor were dismissed,[10] and to underscore the power shift, the praetorian prefecture went to a man who had lost Anastasius' favor eight years earlier, Apion, the scion of a wealthy Egyptian landowning family. But there was no clean sweep: Anastasius' family was untouched, and his nephew Hypatius remained commander in the East until after Justin's death. Celer, who had been a less than enthusiastic supporter of Justin's election, had to give up the powerful post of Master of Offices, but he suffered no harm and continued in the imperial service until his death a few years later. Procopius knew Justin when he was old and ill and thought him in his dotage, but in the initial years of his reign there was no mark of senility. Like the good soldier he had been, he knew how to act decisively and ruthlessly if necessary, but there was nothing vindictive about him.

He had had a remarkable career. He came from Dardania, one of several Latin-speaking provinces in the Balkans and part of the prefecture of Illyricum, which had its seat at Thessaloniki. A horde of Huns under Attila had crossed the Danube in 447 and penetrated as far south as Thermopylae, pillaging as they went, and after Attila's death and the breakup of his horde, it was the Ostrogoths' turn to ravage the area. Settlements were destroyed, and mere survival was hard. When Justin and two companions, Zimarchus and Dityvistus from the little village of Bederiana near modern Skopje, set out about midcentury to find better fortune in the capital, they were not the only provincials to make the journey. They were young Thracians with well-muscled physiques, but the sum total of their possessions was the clothes on their backs and a little hard bread in their pockets. Yet once in Constantinople, they enrolled in the Excubitors, which the emperor Leo I had just created as a new palace guard to counteract the dominance of German soldiery in the capital. We hear no more of Zimarchus and Dityvistus, but Justin rose through the ranks until the emperor Anastasius put him in command of the Excubitors, and from there he stepped into the vacuum of power at Anastasius' death.[11]

As Justin's fortunes rose, he shared them with his family. He brought his sister's son, Flavius Petrus Sabbatius, to the capital and adopted him. We know him by his adopted name, "Justinianus," and if it were not that his consular diptych has survived, we would not have his full name. Justinian was able and ambitious, determined to act as second-in-command as soon as Justin became emperor, but though historians who looked back on the period were to treat Justin's reign as a part of Justinian's, to contemporaries in 518 the succession cannot have seemed quite so assured. Yet Justin needed his adoptive son who had the education he lacked, and his wife, Euphemia, was fond of Justinian too, though she was quite capable of standing up to him if he violated her notion of propriety.

Euphemia is a shadowy figure, though from the scanty evidence we have, she appears to have been a woman of firm convictions whose rise from barbarian slave to empress was almost as remarkable as Theodora's later ascent from the theater to the imperial palace. Procopius tells us almost all we know about her. Justin, he wrote, "lived with a wife whose name was *Loupikine* (Lupicina). She was a slave and a barbarian, and she had been the concubine of her previous owner."[12] Justin, it seems, bought her and wedded her, having first manumitted her, for otherwise he could not have contracted a legal marriage. All this must have happened before Justin reached the rank of senator. She had followed him through his military career for many years before she became empress, when she discarded the name "Lupicina," which smelled of the whorehouse (*lupa* in Latin meant both "prostitute" and "she-wolf"), and adopted the name "Euphemia." It was an interesting choice, a virtuous name hinting at something base, and one source[13] indicates that it was selected by the people when they proclaimed her "Augusta" in the Hippodrome. Like Justin, she was without education or polish, but she was a woman of principle and determined to uphold the dignity of her office. As long as she was alive, she would have nothing to do with Theodora when she became Justinian's concubine. But once Euphemia was dead, Justin was putty in Justinian's hands, and we may speculate that the difference between the vigorous Justin in the early years of his reign and the doddering old man of its latter years was due not merely to ill health and advancing age but also to the absence of his staunch ally, his wife, Euphemia. Their theology coincided. Both were Chalcedonians, and the sharp break with Anastasius' religious policy at the start of Justin's reign reflected Euphemia's convictions as much as it did Justin's or Justinian's.[14]

Anastasius had been a Monophysite; that is, he held to a creed that argued that in Christ there was a single nature that was divine, and while Christ was on earth, he was in fact the Divine Word (*Logos*) appearing as a human being to mankind. The leading Monophysite theologian, Severus, whom Anastasius had appointed patriarch of Antioch, never denied the human nature of Christ, but he refused to separate his human and divine natures. The position of Rome, on the other hand, had been set out in the *Tomus ad Flavianum* of Pope Leo the Great, the notorious "*Tome* of Leo," which was a letter written hastily by the pope and addressed to the patriarch of Antioch, Flavian, at the Second Council of Ephesus, which endorsed Monophysitism. Leo had called it the "Robbers Council," for it was hijacked by the patriarch of Alexandria, and there was no discussion of Leo's *Tome*, which was a bald statement that Christ possessed two natures, one human and the other divine.

Then, two years later, at the Council of Chalcedon (451), there was a reversal. A hunting accident had killed the emperor Theodosius II, and there was a shift of power at court. Theodosius' sister Pulcheria chose the next emperor, and together they swung their support behind Pope Leo's statement of faith. Christ, according to the pronouncement of Chalcedon, was both perfect God and perfect man, consubstantial with the Father in his Godhead and with humanity in his manhood. He was made known to mankind *in* two natures, the properties of which were preserved intact, and both these natures came together to form one person (in Greek, *prosopon*) and one entity (*hypostasis*).

To the Monophysites, this definition was too close for comfort to the heresy of Nestorius, patriarch of Constantinople from 428 until 431, when he was condemned at the first Council of Ephesus. Nestorius had learned his theology as a monk at Antioch, and he emphasized the humanity of Christ to the extent that he objected to the popular epithet for the Virgin: Theotokos (Mother of God). The phrase "*in* two natures" in the Chalcedonian

Creed was a red flag. "*Out of* two natures" might have satisfied the moderate Monophysites, for it avoided offense and did no violence to the teaching of Nestorius' opponent, the great fifth-century patriarch of Alexandria, Cyril, but the phrase "*in* two natures," which Pope Leo supplied, having in turn borrowed it from Saint Augustine, was a rock on which church unity would founder.

The Council of Chalcedon had ended with bitter words. The Chalcedonian Creed split the East and West. It was not a clean split: in Egypt the Pachomian monasteries, that is, those that followed the rule set out by the founder of cenobitic monasticism, Saint Pachomios, were Chalcedonian, and in Palestine there was a brief flirtation with Monophysitism, but then the monasteries edged back toward Chalcedonianism. In the see of Antioch the Chalcedonians held the edge, but their strength was concentrated in the cities, and the hinterland of Antioch became Monophysite and Syriac-speaking. In the villages of Asia Minor, paganism was still strong, and the heresy of Montanism had a significant number of followers in western central Anatolia until Justinian's brutal suppression. A fault line developed between Greco-Roman culture and the ancient civilizations of Egypt and the Near East, and it marked the rupture between the Monophysites and the Chalcedonians.

In 482, during the reign of Zeno, the patriarch Acacius promoted a formula known as the *Henotikon* that tried to satisfy the Monophysites without offending the supporters of the Chalcedonian Creed. It condemned both Nestorius and Eutyches, the founders respectively of Nestorianism and Monophysitism, and anathematized all heresies, "whether advanced at Chalcedon or at any synod whatever." The moderate Monophysites found it acceptable, but Rome would have none of it. The pope excommunicated Acacius, but the imperial court was more interested in keeping the loyalty of Egypt and Syria than in mollifying Rome. It was the provinces in the prefecture of the Orient that filled the treasury with their tax revenues. Not Italy. For thirty-six years, the *Henotikon* remained the touchstone of orthodoxy in the eastern empire, its broad definition providing an umbrella for both Chalcedonian and Monophysite.[15]

But the schism with the papacy hardened. Anastasius had tried hard to find a compromise, but Rome was intransigent, and Anastasius leaned increasingly toward the Monophysites. In 512 he deposed the patriarch of Antioch, Flavian, and exiled him to Petra in the Negev; and in his stead, he appointed the Monophysite, Severus. Severus used his pulpit to promote Monophysitism in the East, though with imperfect success, for in Syria Secunda and Palestine, Chalcedonian doctrine held its own in both the monasteries and most of the cities. In late 517 a group of monks in Syria Secunda went so far as to send a letter to Pope Hormisdas in Rome, whom they addressed as "patriarch of the whole world," and denounced Severus as a heretic in no uncertain terms.[16] In the prefecture of Illyricum where the sees of Rome and Constantinople competed for control, loyalty to Chalcedon was so strong that the Count of the Federate Troops, Vitalian, who was Flavian's godson, got support there for a revolt against Anastasius. He defeated an imperial army at Acra on the Black Sea in 514 and forced Anastasius to reopen negotiations with Pope Hormisdas. But Hormisdas was inflexible, and finally, the year before he died, Anastasius wrote to say that he was not prepared to accept the pope's insults any longer. Vitalian rose in rebellion one last time in 515 and advanced on Constantinople, but this time Anastasius' praetorian prefect, Marinus, defeated his fleet in a battle in which Justin's Excubitors played a significant role.[17] Vitalian had to withdraw. Yet he was still lurking in his native province of Scythia Minor, at the mouth of the Danube, when Justin became emperor, and he remained a threat.[18] One of Justin's first moves was to bring him back to Constantinople and appoint him one of the two Masters of the Soldiers in the Presence.[19] In 520 he made him consul.

Justin had no quarrel with Vitalian's theology, nor did Justinian, though he scented a rival. For them too the pope was the final arbiter of orthodoxy. The decision to yield to the fiat of Rome was Justin's, though Justinian supported it, and so too did the empress Euphemia. Pope Hormisdas was in no mood to make compromises. He sent envoys to Constantinople with instructions to decline any invitation to debate but simply to state Rome's position and demand acquiescence. Justinian was soon to discover that a papal ukase could not achieve theological harmony, but for the moment Rome had its way. The emperors from Zeno to Anastasius and their patriarchs and clergy were declared heretical.

The tide turned in full flood against Monophysitism. Fifty-four bishops were driven from their sees in the prefecture of Oriens. In September 518, a couple of months after Justin's accession, Severus of Antioch, who was warned of his imminent arrest, boarded a ship under cover of night and escaped to Egypt. In the eyes of the Monophysites, he was still patriarch, exile

though he was, but the patriarchal throne of Antioch that he had been forced
to abandon was taken over by an unyielding Chalcedonian, Paul "the Jew,"
whom the pope endorsed. Monophysite monks were hounded out of their
monasteries and persecuted everywhere. The elderly bishop of Hierapolis
(Mabbug), Philoxenus, who, after the patriarch Severus, was the leading
teacher of Monophysitism in Syria and had enjoyed the support of both
Zeno and Anastasius, was exiled and died horribly of suffocation when he
was shut up in a room above the kitchen of a public house.[20]

We have mute evidence from Anatolia: high in the Taurus Mountains
above the Göksu River gorge we may still see the well-preserved ruins of the
Alahan monastery in the heart of ancient Isauria. It was built by monks who
were clearly skilled Isaurian stonemasons. This was Monophysite territory.
Later Chalcedonianism would gain ground here, but at this point Isauria
was loyal to Severus. The monastery was suddenly and mysteriously deserted.
There is no evidence of destruction; yet something forced the monks to leave
and we may well suspect that it was Justin's persecution.[21] Later a group of
monks was to return and make the necessary repairs to the structure, but
they seem to be a new group of holy men, less adept at masonry but possibly
more orthodox in religion.

In Constantinople, Vitalian became a center of power and used his influence to spur on the persecution. He wanted revenge on Severus, the churchman who had replaced his godfather Flavian as patriarch of Antioch. But
he became too powerful for Justinian's taste and in July 520, the year of his
consulship, he was murdered either on his way to the palace or within it. Justinian was blamed, perhaps with grounds, though Vitalian's earlier career as a
pro-Chalcedonian rebel must have made him many enemies who wished him
dead.[22] Justinian took over the office of Master of the Soldiers that Vitalian's
death left vacant.

Egypt remained a safe haven for the refugee churchmen. Pope Hormisdas
had urged Justin to dismiss the patriarch of Alexandria, Timothy III, whose
Monophysite sympathies were well known, and appoint instead a candidate
of the pope's choosing, but Justin, who was willing to follow the pope's di-
rectives elsewhere, balked at interference in Egypt. He treated the see of
Alexandria with circumspection, for Monophysite strength there was daunt-
ing and Alexandria had a long-standing reputation for turbulence. Moreover, grain from the Nile valley fed Constantinople and Egypt's contribution
to the gross domestic product of the empire entitled her to consideration.

Severus, safe in Egypt, remained in exile still the acknowledged leader of the Monophysites, who continued to recognize him as the rightful patriarch of Antioch. Meanwhile his Chalcedonian replacement, Paul "the Jew," persecuted heretical monastics with such cruelty that he was eased off the patriarchal throne, and a more humane Chalcedonian, Euphrasius, took over. The persecution abated somewhat; still, when Euphrasius died horribly in the earthquake and conflagration that followed, which laid Antioch low in 526, the Monophysites considered it a well-deserved death.

Justinian, the Emperor-in-Waiting

Vitalian might be dead, but Justinian was still not completely secure. When his uncle became emperor, he was only a member of the *candidati,* an elite corps of Scholarians who took their name from the white uniforms they wore. Another of Justin's nephews, Germanus, was already winning a military reputation. However, Justinian's advance was rapid; on his accession, Justin made him Count of the Domestics; by the summer of 520 he was one of the two Masters of the Soldiers in the Presence in Constantinople, and in January 521 he became consul and celebrated his inauguration with lavish public games that cost 4,000 gold pounds. He was an ardent aficionado of the "Blues," for as in Rome, the colors Red, White, Blue, and Green marked the four chariot teams that competed in the races in the Hippodrome. By this time, however, the Reds and Whites had become subordinate, and it was the Blues and the Greens that attracted the young men among the urban mob. The Blue and Green factions were the companies that organized not only the chariot races but also theatrical productions—mimes, circus acts, bear baiting, and the like—and their aficionados divided themselves into rival parties whose antagonism animated the public places of the empire's cities.[23] The cohorts of youth who espoused one party or the other were prone to street violence that ebbed and flowed during this period. In Justin's reign public disorder was on the increase, and Justinian was blamed. From 519 on, he cultivated the Blues and acted as their patron. When the Blues committed an outrage, they could rely on Justinian for protection, whereas the Greens were savagely repressed.

It appears that Justinian was attempting to transform the Blues into a personal following that would look to him as their patron. He must have known that his favoritism was encouraging violence in the streets, and yet at this point in his career, which by coincidence was the period when he met his future wife, Theodora, and she became his concubine, he seems to have thought that a feeling of insecurity in the capital would further his objectives. Procopius noted that not all the Blues were willing to follow Justinian's lead, but among them there was a hawkish group that did, and their counterparts among the Greens responded in kind. They dressed like Huns, wearing untrimmed beards and moustaches and hair clipped short in front but long at the back, and they sported expensive clothes, with loosely fitted sleeves to accommodate their impressive biceps, or so, sneered Procopius, they would have liked people to imagine! Respectable citizens, including moderate Blues, were outraged and even frightened by these street gangs, and there was a hint of revolution in the air. Some moneylenders were so alarmed that they forgave debts, and there were slave owners who thought it prudent to free their slaves.[24] Those senatorial families whose influence had diminished in the new regime after Anastasius' death must have felt particularly apprehensive. The rich and aristocratic Anicia Juliana, a descendant of the House of Theodosius, lavished her wealth on the construction of the great church of Saint Polyeuktos, the largest church in Constantinople until Justinian built the cathedral of Hagia Sophia. A tradition known to Gregory of Tours indicates that she built it as her palace chapel to keep her fortune out of Justinian's covetous hands.[25]

The violence got out of hand, however, and in 523 a citizen of Constantinople named Hypatius was killed in Hagia Sophia itself. The murder was reported to Justin, who had been unaware of how much the violence had escalated, and he was incensed. He instructed the urban prefect Theodore "Colocynthius" (the Pumpkin) to restore order. Theodore acted vigorously. Blue malefactors were hanged or burned alive. Justinian was seriously ill at the time, and while his life was in danger, he could not interfere. But once he recovered he took revenge on the unfortunate urban prefect, who was exiled and forced to seek refuge in a monastery to escape assassination. Thereafter the violence abated for a while,[26] and once Justinian became co-emperor with his uncle in 527, he sent rescripts to all the cities ordering no more riots or murders and directing that troublemakers should be punished with an even hand, Blues and Greens alike.[27]

The Blues were the smaller party and ordinarily the more moderate.[28] Their ranks may have attracted the landowners and rentiers, whereas the more numerous Greens were the party of preference for the traders and artisans, some with family connections in Syria and possibly with greater sympathy for the Monophysitism preached by Severus, the charismatic patriarch of Antioch whom Justin ousted.[29] However, the view that was once accepted, that the Greens supported Monophysitism whereas the Blues were Chalcedonian, does not survive examination. Neither party gave consistent support for one variety of religious dogma or the other. The old emperor Anastasius, who was Monophysite, favored the Reds, which was next best to being neutral, and the reason for his diplomatic partisanship may have been that he considered neither of the larger parties reliable supporters of his brand of theology. Justinian's motive for supporting the Blues may have been based on the principle that by favoring the smaller, weaker party, he could make it part of his clientage. However, Theodora's devotion to the Blues rested on a family tie that historians never guessed until a manuscript of Procopius' *Anekdota* was discovered in the Vatican Library and published in 1623. Theodora's attachment went back to her childhood and is proof that loyalty to the Blues and allegiance to Monophysite theology were not antithetical.

The Early Life of Theodora

Theodora's Beginning

Theodora's father, Acacius, was the bear keeper for the Greens at the Hippodrome in Constantinople. We know nothing about him, but a tradition related by the ninth-century patriarch, Nicephoros, makes him a native of Cyprus.[1] Nicephoros tells a story that when Justinian made his own birthplace an archbishopric and called it "Justiniana Prima," he also made Cyprus an independent archbishopric named "Justiniana Secunda" as a favor for Theodora, who came from there. This piece of information sounds like an ingenious explanation for the title borne by the head of the Cypriote church: "Archbishop of Nova Justiniana and all Cyprus."[2] In fact, Cyprus was already an independent archbishopric by Justinian's day; Theodora had nothing to do with it. The archbishop's title derives from a futile attempt of Justinian II in 691 to transplant the Cypriotes to a settlement named "Nova Justinianopolis" on the Hellespont, a venture he abandoned seven years later, and only the title "Archbishop of Nova Justiniana[3] and all Cyprus" survives to commemorate it. Yet a Cypriote birthplace fitted the romantic legend of Theodora, for classical mythology told that the goddess of love and sexual passion, Aphrodite, was born there. It was appropriate that the courtesan who inflamed the passion of the middle-aged Justinian should have been born there too. Probably she was a native of Constantinople, and the origin of her family is an open question.

Acacius fathered three daughters, Comito, Theodora, and Anastasia, but he died before the eldest, Comito, reached the age of seven.[4] His death need not have been a calamity if he had had a grown son to take up his vocation, for the post of bear keeper for the Greens would have passed to him, but as it was, the little family faced destitution. Theodora's mother remarried hastily, hoping that her new husband would take over Acacius' job. But in the Green faction, it was the head ballet dancer, Asterius, whose right it was to make the decision, and he accepted a bribe from another candidate and appointed him. Desperate, Theodora's mother played her final card. She presented her daughters as suppliants before the spectators in the Hippodrome, with garlands on their heads, and begged the Greens for compassion. But the Greens showed no interest. The Blues, however, had just lost their bear keeper, and the position was open. They took pity on the penniless family and gave the post to Theodora's stepfather. Theodora did not forget the kindness of the Blues.

Of the various comedy forms inherited from the Roman theater, only the mime still flourished,[5] and its specialty was off-color slapstick. Actors and actresses were the dregs of society, particularly those women who cavorted in the theater orchestras, which might be waterproofed and flooded so that they could play water games, clad in revealing bathing suits. "Swimming whores" John Chrysostom[6] had called them in a homily he delivered at Antioch in 390. A street in Constantinople's theater district bore the name Pornai:[7] "Harlots' Row" would be an acceptable translation, and the implication is plain.

In the civilian hierarchy, the personnel of both the theater and the Hippodrome ranked at the bottom of the social pyramid. Churchmen denounced them, and they were denied the sacraments unless they were on their deathbeds. Even then the law required that the danger of death be extreme, and the bishop and chief city officials had to investigate and approve before the last rites were granted, for once an actor had received the sacraments, he could not be recalled to the theater,[8] and the shows had to go on. Performers might be despised and rejected of men, but their services were deemed necessary. The mob had to be amused. Mimes were recommended as interludes between chariot races in the hippodromes of the empire, for they gave pleasure without kindling passions and they soothed the emotions of the spectators.[9]

Like other tradesmen, actors and actresses were bound by law to their vocation. An actress might petition for release in the name of religion, claiming that she wanted to enter a convent, and stage performers who were redeemed from the theater and became ascetics made a favorite subject for Christian texts. But if the penitent actress was caught indulging in "indecent embraces" after her release from the stage, the law demanded that she be dragged back to it, to perform until she grew to be an ugly old woman.[10] Even then she would be denied absolution, however much her wrinkled face and unappetizing body might leave her no choice other than chastity. For women such as Theodora and her sisters, the alternatives were the stage or the convent. They chose the stage, or, perhaps to be more accurate, their mother made the choice for them.

Comito soon became a star. Theodora made her stage debut as her sister's attendant, dressed as a slave girl. Procopius,[11] who is our only source for Theodora's life as an actress, claims that even at this early age she submitted to the buggery of slaves who accompanied their masters to the theater, but once she matured into a woman she became a prostitute. The mentality of the age assumed that all actresses were trollops, and even if Theodora had not sold her favors, it would have been taken for granted that she did. Yet there is no reason to think her an exception to the rule.[12] She had nothing to sell except a lovely body, for she could neither dance nor play an instrument, and when she did make an attempt to entertain at banquets, the only act she could offer was a striptease. But she was a gifted comedienne, and her specialty in the theater was the comic mime. She was famous for her performance of "Leda and the Swan." Naked, except for a girdle, she reclined onstage while some slaves sprinkled barley over her groin, and a small gaggle of trained geese waddled up and picked the grains off her with their beaks. Once the act was finished, Theodora got to her feet and acknowledged the applause. "She got to her feet without so much as a blush," reported the *Secret History.* "[I]ndeed she seemed to take great pride in this performance of hers." [13] It seems she was also a contortionist who could bend her back until her mouth was level with her groin. Procopius invites our disapproval.

The stories Procopius relates about Theodora's early life in his *Secret History* may be only half-true, and fitted out with much embellishment, but they are representative of the gossip that floated through the streets of the capital. They were heard with relish by the old ruling classes who both scorned and feared her once she became empress. Her sexual appetite was insatiable, it was reported, and her specialty was young males who had not yet grown their first beards. One story, which sounds like a tale from the men's locker room, related that she would go to banquets with ten young men or more, all experienced fornicators, and exhaust them all, whereupon she would service their attendants, who might number thirty. This sort of incident, which Procopius [14] suggests happened more than once, sounds more like gang rape than a case of nymphomania, and gang rapes must have been a not uncommon hazard of an actress's profession.

A century ago, Charles Diehl,[15] a gallant defender of Theodora, asked pertinently how Procopius learned all the stories about Theodora that he relates. People who valued their reputations avoided her in the marketplace, the *Secret History* reports.[16] Particularly in the morning. Probably some of these lurid details floated about the whorehouses of the capital, where Procopius himself may have been an occasional customer. John Julius Norwich, who calls Procopius a "sanctimonious old hypocrite" who clearly relished every word he wrote in the *Secret History,* goes on to admit that Theodora was "no better than she should have been. Whether she was more depraved than others of her sort is open to question."[17] But, to answer Diehl's question, what Procopius reports was for the most part hearsay. And the *Secret History* gives us a portion of the malevolent rumors about Theodora's early life that circulated behind her back in upper-class circles.

She did have a bastard daughter whose name is unknown, and possibly a son, for Procopius[18] reports gossip about a youth named John who arrived in Constantinople and claimed that his father, on his deathbed, told him his mother was the empress and that if he had not snatched him away, she would have killed him at birth. His tale reached Theodora, who summoned him and had him spirited away to someplace where no one might find him. He was never seen again, not even after Theodora died. The story sounds unlikely, for why should Theodora have acknowledged a bastard daughter and refused a son? "John" sounds like an impostor, if he existed at all.

Then Theodora found a deliverer, or so she thought. She caught the attention of Hecebolus,[19] a native of Tyre whose sole claim to fame is that Theodora was for a brief period his concubine. When he was appointed governor of the Libyan Pentapolis in Africa, she went with him. A man of his standing could disregard the law forbidding the abduction of an actress from the stage and keeping her in his house.[20] But he soon discarded Theodora. Perhaps he found her reputation embarrassing,[21] or—more likely—he wanted a mistress who was meek as well as beautiful, and meekness was never one of Theodora's qualities. But Theodora, having escaped the theater, was in no hurry to return to it. She made her way to Alexandria. Procopius implies that she made her living practicing the only profession she knew, but if she did so, she did it with reluctance. For in Alexandria, it seems she was converted.

The date cannot have been much later than Justin's accession. Alexandria had become a refuge for Monophysite churchmen forced into exile once their protector Anastasius was dead, and the policy of the new emperor veered sharply toward Chalcedonian orthodoxy and reconciliation with Rome. But the see of Saint Mark had enough power and wealth to make any imperial governor think twice before joining battle with it. The Alexandrian populace was volatile and produced a bountiful crop of fanatics. We do not know what religious sympathies Theodora may have had earlier, and as an actress she could not have been baptized, but in Alexandria she must have encountered an assortment of Monophysite churchmen. Years later the author of the Arabic *Liber Pontificalis*[22] of the Alexandrian patriarchate, Severus of Ashmounein, was actually to claim Theodora as an Alexandrian: Alexandria, he reported, was the city whence she had originally come. A Coptic[23] tradition indicates that she met the patriarch Timothy III himself and accepted him as her spiritual father. She may have become a catechumen, for at this time adults might be enrolled in the catechumenate even though they did not intend to seek baptism in the immediate future. It was an immense leap across the gulf that separated an actress from a catechumen, and for Theodora perhaps not yet possible. Still, it may have been in Alexandria that she discovered a new respect for the company of holy men and women, for in her later life as empress she sheltered an assortment of uncouth, fanatical monks, clergy, solitaries, and pillar saints and sought their blessings and discussed theology with them. She became an enthusiastic amateur theologian, and her devotion to Monophysitism was never to waver.

From Alexandria Theodora went to Antioch. She had not abandoned her connections with the Blues, for when she reached Antioch, still smarting at her treatment by Hecebolus, she met a dancing girl named Macedonia who was employed by the Blue faction. Macedonia had a dual career: she was not only a dancer but also an informer, an agent of Justinian who passed on intelligence about enemies of the regime. The theatrical profession must have been a good recruiting ground for informers, though we get only occasional glimpses of the network of spies and runners who gleaned intelligence for the court. The *Life* of Saint Theodore of Sykeon[24] supplies one example: Cosmas, an acrobat (or perhaps a retired acrobat) from the Hippodrome who served as Justinian's courier. He sired Theodore in the course of a night he spent in Sykeon at an inn kept by Theodore's mother, his aunt, and his grandmother, who supplemented their income by prostitution. It appears that Macedonia recruited Theodora into Justinian's service.

From Procopius[25] we have only a sketchy account, but it takes very little imagination to fill in the details. Macedonia found Theodora dejected not only because she was a discarded mistress with no prospects but also because she had just lost some money. Macedonia told her that her fortune would change, and Theodora in turn recalled that the night before she had had a dream that told her to have no worries about money, for she would arrive at Constantinople and there she would sleep with the Lord of the Demons who would bring her wealth. We may leave aside the apocalyptic element, for the thesis of the *Secret History* is that Justinian and his empress were the Antichrist. The core of the story suggests that Macedonia was the go-between who brought Theodora to Justinian's attention as a useful contact, and Justinian, who was already approaching middle age, fell in love. Theodora became his mistress, living with him in the Palace of Hormisdas. By 523 he had raised her to the rank of patrician.[26]

For this story we depend on Procopius, and he is a malevolent witness. There were other legends with a loftier moral tone. A late source relates a story that when Justinian discovered Theodora, she was a poor girl from Paphlagonia, living virtuously in a humble house in Constantinople and supporting herself by spinning wool, and that when she became empress she built the church of Saint Panteleëmon, the "All-Merciful," where her house once stood.[27] Behind this tale we may recognize dimly the story pattern of the redeemed actress who abandoned the theater for a virtuous life. Procopius, who reports the building of Saint Panteleëmon, does not connect Theodora with the church.[28] Yet Procopius' omission may not prove that Theodora had nothing to do with it, for devotion to the All-Merciful saint would have fitted her public image very well.

In the East, where Theodora was remembered warmly as the patron of the Jacobite church, there was another legend.[29] Theodora was the daughter of a Monophysite cleric either at Callinicum (Raqqa) or at Hierapolis (Mabbug), and Justinian met her while he was campaigning there as Justin's Master of the Soldiers. He fell in love, but Theodora's father would not consent to the marriage until Justinian swore that he would never make Theodora assent to the Creed of Chalcedon. Then Justinian returned to Constantinople and three months later Justin died. Both stories are evidence of the high regard that the Jacobite church had for her. But they are not history. Yet there are two scraps of evidence that support the story the *Secret History* tells about Theodora's early career.

One comes from the Syriac churchman and historian, John of Ephesus. He was a friend of Theodora and considered her little short of a saint. In his *Lives of the Eastern Saints* he presents a vivid picture of the Monophysite ascetics in the East and their travails during the persecutions of Justin and Justinian. He devoted a *Life* to certain clergy in the retinue of Mare,[30] the metropolitan bishop of Amida and a Monophysite, who was expelled from his see, and in it he tells how the bishop sent his deacon and notary, Stephen, to Constantinople to intercede with the authorities. He directed him especially to "Theodora *who came from the brothel* [the phrase is Greek] and was at that time a patrician and eventually became queen."[31] She was not yet Justinian's wedded wife, but she was his concubine, and Justinian was Master of the Soldiers. She was already known to have influence. John of Ephesus was a friendly witness, without Procopius' animus or prurience, and we may take him as an honest reporter. John inserted Greek phrases into his Syriac text not infrequently, for he was bilingual to the extent that he thought in both languages,[32] but the epithet "who came from the brothel" may not have been his coinage. Rather it was common usage among Constantinople's hoi polloi. They knew Theodora's past. Her life in the theater cannot have been a secret, and theaters and brothels went together. But in contemporary Christian thought, it was not the sins of the past but penitence that mattered. With similar transparency, the hagiography of Saint Theodore of Sykeon reports without embarrassment that the saint's mother had been a part-time courtesan and his father a transient customer.

The other shred of evidence is a law of Justin, which—though it mentions no names—was designed to remove all legal obstacles in the way of a marriage between Justinian and Theodora. It leaves no doubt that Theodora came from the theater.[33]

The marriage had to circumvent two obstacles. One was Justin's wife, the empress Euphemia. She would have nothing to do with Theodora. Theodora was already known for her Monophysite sympathies, which Euphemia, a stout Chalcedonian, must have found disturbing. Moreover, her own elevation to empress had made her a respectable woman, and respectable women did not go to the theater, much less receive actresses into their families. While his wife was alive, Justin deferred to her and refused to facilitate the marriage of Justinian and Theodora. But Justinian did not have long to wait; Euphemia must have been dead by 524,[34] and old Justin without his wife was malleable.

But the law was still an obstacle. An edict of the emperor Constantine the Great forbade marriage between senators and actresses or daughters of actresses. Justinian persuaded Justin to issue a new law. Its date is 524 at the latest, and it was a comprehensive regulation [35] that allowed actresses who had abandoned their dishonorable profession and sincerely repented to marry a man of high station with the emperor's permission. Indeed, the emperor's permission would be unnecessary if the women were already raised to the rank of patrician, and Theodora already was a patrician. Daughters of actresses likewise had restrictions removed. Procopius [36] grumbled that the law allowed any man who wished to, to marry a courtesan. Some did: Theodora's sister Comito made a good marriage to Sittas, a promising army officer, and Theodora's good friend Antonina, whose father was a charioteer and mother one of the low-class performers who danced in the theater orchestras, married Belisarius, who at the time was probably still one of Justinian's guardsmen. Possibly it was Belisarius' marriage, which was almost as unorthodox as Justinian's, that caused him to be noticed.

Theodora herself arranged a match for her bastard daughter with a scion of the house of the old emperor Anastasius.[37] The enactment was made retroactive, so that a father could make children born from a union with an actress his legitimate heirs. The law went far beyond what was needed to legitimize the marriage of Theodora and Justinian. It annihilated a significant class barrier. Procopius was not far wrong in his assessment of its effects.

Theodora and Justinian were duly wedded, perhaps in 525.[38] By then Theodora had been living with Justinian in the Palace of Hormisdas near the Julian harbor on the Sea of Marmara for at least two years. She had become a person of influence. She had already intervened on behalf of the Monophysite refugees in answer to the appeal of Mare, bishop of Amida.[39] Theodora would never be a meek or silent partner.

By 527 Justin's health was failing rapidly, and on April 1, three days before Easter, he crowned Justinian co-emperor and Augustus in the great Tricilinium of the Nineteen Couches in the palace, and at the same time he crowned Theodora. On Easter Day, in the great basilica of Hagia Sophia built by the emperor Theodosius II, the patriarch performed the coronation ceremony and administered the oath. Then the new rulers of the empire made their way in solemn procession, accompanied by the palace guards, to the Hippodrome, where they showed themselves in the *kathisma* and received the acclamations of the people.[40] Theodora, who had begun her life on the stage and had belonged to the dregs of society, was now acclaimed Theodora Augusta. Not a single member of the senate expressed disapproval, Procopius reported with indignation. No priest showed any sign of outrage. The people, who had attended her performances in the theater, now clamored to be her subjects. It was, Procopius[41] suggested, an exhibition of Tyche, that is, Fortune, which even in a Christian world exalted and debased persons for no rhyme or reason. Theodora had been lucky.

We may wonder what she herself felt. Exultation, possibly. Gratitude for the providence of God, probably, for she was devout. Yet perhaps she too reflected on the power of Fortune, which had raised up the little girl who had once stood with her two sisters as a suppliant in the Hippodrome and pleaded in vain for compassion from the Greens. Fortune had brought her to the same Hippodrome and raised her to the lofty rank of Augusta, enthroned in the imperial loge and receiving the acclamations of the people who once snickered at her performance in "Leda and the Swan." Only four months later Justin was to die, and Justinian became sole emperor with Theodora his associate in power. "Our most reverend partner granted Us by God," he calls her in one of his laws,[42] and when provincial governors took their oaths of allegiance, the oath that was prescribed for them pledged loyalty to Justinian *and* to Theodora.[43]

Theodora Despoinis

Theodora was now empress with all the emblems of rank that went with the office; yet she did not forget her beginnings or snub her old friends from the theater. She welcomed them into the palace. Procopius reports three old friends who had lodgings there, one named Indaro and the other two with the popular stage name Chrysomallo (Goldilocks). Their names advertised their blond hair, natural or artificial.[44] Procopius makes the nasty but unlikely insinuation that they carried on their old profession from the palace address. Theodora looked after the interests of these entertainers and found husbands for their daughters. This was behavior that the upper classes found shocking, and perhaps it was intended to shock. Theodora was not prepared to respect the social niceties of the past that had disadvantaged women, particularly women who came from the class to which she had once belonged.

Theodora did not forget the snubs and slights she had once suffered. The old elite of the capital regarded this new imperial pair, the one sprung from Thracian peasants and the other from the theater, with concealed disdain, and Justinian, who was more good-natured than his wife, might shrug it off. Not so Theodora. A patrician who was hounded by his creditors and could not pay them because he was unable to collect the debts he was owed once tried to get Theodora's help. He assumed the mien of a suppliant in tears and approached her in the women's quarters of the palace. Theodora and her attendants ridiculed him. We have the story from Procopius[45] of how they staged an impromptu mime for him, in which the patrician found himself cast unwillingly in the role of an ugly old man entreating courtesans for favors. No doubt Procopius has omitted relevant details. The patrician may have made Theodora's acquaintance before she became empress and snubbed her, and if not he, then others of his ilk. Seeing him prostrate before her was sweet revenge.

Protocol became important as never before. Theodora was exigent in her demand for every courtesy an empress could rightfully expect. Hitherto, when senators entered the imperial presence, the patricians stooped and touched the emperor's right breast with their lips and the emperor kissed their heads and sent them on their way. The other senators merely genuflected. But with Justinian and Theodora, all senators, whatever their rank, had to prostrate themselves face downward on the floor and with their lips touch the imperial feet not only of Justinian but of Theodora as well.[46] Never before had an empress received such an honor. It was not enough to address her as "Basilis" (empress) and Justinian as "Basileus" (emperor); the titles "Despoinis" and "Despotes" (Mistress and Master) were now de rigueur. Ceremonial, much of it borrowed from the Persian monarchy, was already at home in the imperial court, but with Justinian and Theodora it became the symbol of absolutism, marking off this imperial pair with their lowly origins as the chosen representatives of Heaven. The regime's severest critic, Procopius, noted the change and was censorious.[47] The distance between the emperor and empress and their subjects was emphasized; even the imperial loge in the Hippodrome was remodeled to make it loftier and more effulgent than before.[48] It is no wonder that Peter the Patrician, Master of Offices from 539 until his death twenty-six years later, whose duties included implementing the new ceremonial, wrote a manual on it that survives at second hand in the tenth-century *De Caerimoniis* (On Ceremonial Procedures) by the emperor Constantine Porphyrogenitus. Theodora's enemy, the praetorian prefect for the East, John the Cappadocian, who preferred efficiency to ceremony and pruned the formalities of the prefect's office, watched with a disdain that Theodora sensed and added to her list of reasons for hating him.

A contemporary portrait of her still gazes down on us from the side wall of the chancel of San Vitale in Ravenna, facing her husband on the opposite wall. The church was dedicated only shortly before she died of cancer.[49] Her great eyes and her oval, rather severe face arrest the onlooker. She is surrounded by her attendants, and though she was a petite woman, she dominates the composition. Procopius left two descriptions, both written after her death in 548. In his unpublished *Secret History* that expresses the suppressed rage of the Constantinople elite, he allows her an attractive appearance, but she was short and her complexion was pale and a little sallow. Her gaze was intense. The great eyes of the Ravenna portrait were copied from life. But Procopius' second description, which we find in his encomium on Justinian's building program, is rather different. There, as we might expect, Theodora was depicted as a woman of indescribable beauty.[50]

She had left poverty behind her, and now she lived the life of a wealthy, respectable Roman lady. She took great care to preserve an attractive appearance. Procopius[51] thought she bewitched her husband. The relationship between the two was a remarkable one, for she was not only her husband's partner in power but also his loyal opposition. In the senate, Justinian and Theodora would argue questions from different viewpoints while the senators listened, but it was suspected that they agreed beforehand which of them would win the debate. The senators themselves had nothing to say; they provided merely a colorful background.[52] On matters of faith, Theodora was the patron of the Monophysites while Justinian defended orthodoxy. Did they agree to disagree? Their subjects were puzzled. Here is Procopius, whose perspective is rancorous:

> Now first they set the Christians at each other's throats, and by pretending to go in opposite directions in the questions under debate, they thus split the whole populace into two groups.[53]

Procopius thought that Justinian and Theodora advertised a simulated contention as part of a diabolic scheme to ruin the empire. But Evagrius, writing at the end of the century, was merely baffled by them:

Justinian maintained the synod of Chalcedon with utmost steadfastness, and Theodora his consort sided with those who upheld the single nature, either because those were their real beliefs—for when faith is in dispute, fathers are divided against their offspring, and their offspring against those who gave them birth, a wife against her own husband and a husband against his wife—or by an understanding between them that he should champion those who upheld the two natures of Christ our Lord after the union, and she those who claimed a single nature. Neither yielded to the other.[54]

Yet there was statecraft behind their disagreement. As long as the Monophysites had a friend in court, they continued to owe their allegiance to the empire, and dialogue between the two poles of religious belief that split the Christian world could continue. But there was personal difference as well. Theodora's commitment to Monophysite dogma was sincere, and it did not alter, but Justinian, one senses, was less certain. The aim of his incursions into theology was to discover an area of agreement between the Chalcedonians and the Monophysites, but it is also true that he passionately loved the intellectual cut and thrust of theological dispute. He continued to rethink his position; in the last year of his reign he shifted from orthodoxy to extreme Monophysitism.[55] Theodora was by then long dead. Yet Justinian's memories of his debates with her may have had a delayed effect. She had sown doubts in his mind, and they finally bore fruit.

At any rate, once Theodora became Augusta, she had a brief window of opportunity to put her mark on Christendom, and she used it as far as she was able. Her resolute hands were now on the levers of power.

The Early Years in Power

The New Augusta

The great propylaeum of the Daphne Palace where the emperors lived was destroyed by fire in the Nika revolt of 532, and it was rebuilt magnificently by Justinian as part of a building program that transformed the heart of Constantinople. It was a domed building, known as the Khalke (the Brazen House), either because it had bronze roof tiles or because it had gates made of bronze. The underside of its dome was decorated with a famous mosaic celebrating the conquests of the reign. There Justinian was shown victorious in the conquest of Africa and in Italy through the campaigns of his general Belisarius. In the center of the composition were the figures of Justinian and Theodora, shown rejoicing in victory, and round about them stood the senators, jubilant and laudatory. The archetypal good emperor of Late Antiquity was one on whom God bestowed victory. *Tu vincas,* "May you be victorious," were the words with which the people acclaimed a new emperor in the Hippodrome. But the mosaic decorating the dome of the Brazen House showed not only a victorious emperor; beside him, sharing the victory, and its mystique, was the empress.

The Vandal expedition had been the first great military success of Justinian's regime. A modest force of eighteen thousand men led by Belisarius sailed from Constantinople in 533, about the time of the summer solstice, made an unopposed landing on the east coast of modern Tunisia, and with two pitched battles overthrew the Vandal kingdom. The Vandal king, Gelimer, was brought to Constantinople, together with a vast amount of loot, including the treasures from the Temple in Jerusalem. The treasures had been taken by Romans when they captured Jerusalem and destroyed the Temple in A.D. 70, and they were in turn stolen from the Forum of Peace in Rome when the Vandals plundered the city in 455. In earlier centuries when Roman armies regularly won victories, conquering generals had been honored with triumphs: the victor paraded his captives and his plunder down the Sacred Way through the Roman Forum, while he himself brought up the rear, making his way to the temple of Jupiter Optimus Maximus on the Capitoline Hill where he formally laid down his command. After the conquest of the Vandal kingdom, the Roman Empire held a triumph for the last time. The parade began at Belisarius' house and made its way to the Hippodrome to salute the emperor and empress. But Belisarius walked; the traditional chariot that used to carry a triumphant general would not do. This was an autocracy where victorious commanders, however brilliant their victories, were still subjects of the emperor and empress.

The parade entered the Hippodrome, filled to capacity, and proceeded to the imperial loge where Justinian and Theodora sat in majesty. Together Belisarius and Gelimer prostrated themselves before the emperor and empress. The victory belonged to the emperor, but he shared it with his empress. They were partners in this as in all else. The mosaic in the Brazen House conveyed the same message as the triumph. It was reported that when Gelimer saw the applauding crowds and the imperial partners in their loge, he muttered over and over again sotto voce the verse from Ecclesiastes: "Vanity of vanities, all is vanity."[1]

The extent to which Justinian and Theodora advertised their partnership surprised contemporaries and attracted comment after their deaths. This was not so much a monarchy as a dyarchy, observed the twelfth-century Byzantine theologian and historian John Zonaras,[2] who surmised that of the two, Theodora may have had the greater power. Both Justinian and Theodora were named in the oath of loyalty that imperial officials were required to take. Justinian acknowledged that he consulted her.[3] She received foreign ambassadors and acted, Procopius complained, as if she bestrode the whole empire.[4] "Theodora," wrote John Julius Norwich, taking Procopius at his word, "was to be no Empress Consort, spending her life quietly with her attendant ladies in the *gynaeceum,* and appearing with her husband only on the most solemn occasions."[5]

Yet Norwich's judgment needs some qualification. Imperial women before Theodora had carved out spaces for themselves. She did not have far to look for models to copy. In the Augustaeum, the square in front of Hagia Sophia, stood a column bearing a likeness of the emperor Constantine's mother, the

Augusta Helena, and in the northeast corner of the same square there was a column with a silver statue of the empress Eudoxia, who was a power to be reckoned with at the court of Arcadius. The dowager empress Verina engineered a coup that drove her son-in-law, the emperor Zeno, into exile for a brief period, and in 491 Ariadne, Zeno's widow, chose Anastasius to succeed her husband, and her choice was accepted even though the patriarch was distressed by Anastasius' Monophysite reputation. Theodora never attained the power of these women. Her image never appeared on Justinian's coinage. Nor had Euphemia's on old Justin's, but earlier empresses had enjoyed the honor, and the wife of Justinian's successor, Justin II, who was Theodora's niece Sophia, appears on her husband's coins. Not Theodora.

Her power was secondhand. If she was influential, it was because Justinian respected her. It was not merely that he was deeply in love, though that was true. Rather he realized early that Theodora was a shrewd ally, and her experience allowed her to understand the forces that drove public opinion in the eastern part of the empire, which we must balance against her failure to comprehend the mind-set of the West. Justinian never doubted her loyalty, even when she might act with a degree of independence that is surprising. She was bound to him both by affection and by self-interest. Moreover, Justinian realized, one suspects, that it was an advantage for an autocrat to have a secondary power center in the state so long as it was firmly in the hands of a loyal wife. Theodora served as His Majesty's loyal opposition.

Like earlier emperors and empresses, Theodora cultivated a public image. She was to have her counterpart of the empress Eudoxia's column, though its placement was less conspicuous. It was a porphyry shaft bearing her statue that stood in the courtyard of the Arcadian Baths. Procopius,[6] writing after Theodora's death, speaks in flattering tones of the statue's beauty, which, he claimed, fell short of reality. Justinian built the colonnaded courtyard beside the sea to provide public urban space, but it was the city of Constantinople that erected the column out of gratitude to Theodora, Procopius reported. The column implied that the people recognized Theodora as their benefactor, and she may have deserved the recognition. A park for the masses packed into the crowded city of Constantinople fitted her public image. For Theodora decided early what reputation she wanted to cultivate, and it was one befitting her background. She wanted to be known for more than piety and good works. Her special concern would be for the unfortunate.

She was "the God-crowned Theodora whose mind is adorned with piety and whose constant toil lies in unsparing efforts to nourish the destitute."[7] The quotation comes from the great inscription on the architrave beneath the dome of Saints Sergius and Bacchus, which still stands close to the old Bucoleon harbor on the Sea of Marmara, separated from the shore by an elevated railway. Its present name is Küçük Aya Sofya Camii: the mosque of Little Hagia Sophia, for its architecture resembles the great church of Hagia Sophia, which it antedates by a few years, though there is a closer model in Ravenna's church of San Vitale, which is its contemporary. Justinian built Saints Sergius and Bacchus when he became emperor, north of the earlier church of Saints Peter and Paul that he built while Justin was still on the throne. The two shared a narthex.[8] Both churches were part of the Palace of Hormisdas, where Justinian and Theodora lived until Justin died, and after Justinian became emperor he enclosed it within the imperial palace precincts. Theodora was to turn it into a refuge for Monophysite saints, and possibly Saints Sergius and Bacchus became their church, while Saints Peter and Paul became the church for the Latin rite. Theodora's monogram does not appear on the interior capitals of Saints Sergius and Bacchus as it does in Hagia Sophia and Hagia Eirene, which were built after the conflagration of 532, but the great inscription below the dome, although it names Justinian alone as the builder, nonetheless concludes with her manifesto. She sought a reputation as a compassionate Augusta whose special concern was the hapless and the needy.

Her kindness was remembered. The church historian Evagrius,[9] who wrote after her death and did not share her theology, nonetheless records that she was kind to "our people." "Our people" must refer to the Antiochenes, since Evagrius was a lawyer in Antioch, or it may have the broader sense of the provincials in the East. But at least he did not mean the Monophysites, whom Theodora supported, for Evagrius was a Chalcedonian and the Monophysites were not *his* people. Clearly Theodora's compassion transcended theological animosity, and Evagrius recognized it.

Theodora's public persona meshed well with Justinian's. Previous emperors had paraded the conventional virtues. The first of them, Augustus, was presented with a golden shield on which was inscribed what were to become the imperial virtues: *virtus* (hardihood), *clementia* (forbearance), *pietas* (devotion), and *iustitia* (justice). Piety acquired Christian overtones in Late Antiquity, though its connotations recalled an earlier pagan world. The piety of Justinian and Theodora was emphasized in official inscriptions. But the salient virtue to which Justinian laid claim in his laws was *philanthropia,* which cannot be translated by the English word "philanthropy." Its meaning is "loving concern for humanity," and it was coupled with piety (*eusebeia*). It was the moral basis of Justinian's imperial office, which he had received from God, and as a deacon of Hagia Sophia reminded him in an essay that he presented to him early in his reign, an emperor's duty was to emulate the mercy of God since his empire was an imitation of God's.[10] He had received absolute power from God, and Theodora, whose power derived from Justinian's, cultivated her husband's virtues at second hand. But her *philanthropia* had a definite focus. She would defend those who could not defend themselves.

She had known poverty and a life beyond the pale, and she did not forget. She wanted wealth and honor, and Justinian was a generous lover. The empress Euphemia may have prevented him from marrying Theodora until after her death, but she could not stop him from bestowing riches on her. For the first time in her life, Theodora had more than enough money. She acquired a fortune.[11] She received still more as a marriage donation, and when she became empress, she acquired the properties that were an empress's portion. There were estates in Pontus, Paphlagonia, and Cappadocia, all administered by her own business manager, or *curator.*[12] Transfers of property from Justinian to Theodora, or vice versa, were ruled to be beyond public scrutiny. Justinian claimed this imperial privilege for himself and his consort, for why should they not have a prerogative worthy of their own fortune, when they labor day and night by their own counsels and by their own labors for the whole world?[13] Why, indeed?

She must have longed for luxury in her impoverished childhood, and now it was hers to enjoy. She reveled in it. In the morning she took a long bath; then she had breakfast followed by a little rest. For luncheon and dinner her table was loaded with fine food and drink.[14] She may have admired ascetics, but a life of asceticism was not for her. She was vain about her beauty and took great care to avoid fatigue. In the summer she regularly retired to a palace at Hieron at the exit from the Bosporus into the Black Sea, where by coincidence there was a customshouse to control trade. The place was difficult to provision, and Theodora's attendants suffered great hardship, Procopius[15] complained, and no doubt he took care not to minimize their tribulations.

In 529 she visited the spa at Pythia in Bithynia, where there were hot springs. She wanted to conceive and have a child by Justinian, and it is not wild imagination to think that concern for her general health took her there. But the extravagance of her expedition made an impression. She traveled with a retinue of four thousand patricians, eunuchs of the bedchamber, and other staff including the chief finance minister, the Count of the Sacred Largesses, to look after expenditures. It was a vulgar display of wealth. Along the way, Theodora made generous donations to churches, monasteries, and hospices, and for her comfort Justinian built a palace and an aqueduct in the town itself.[16] She was doing what wealthy women had done before her to mark their social distinction, and for an erstwhile burlesque queen whom the upper classes had disdained, it must have been a very gratifying thing to do.

Theodora was acquisitive not merely for herself. She looked after the interests of her family and her old friends and secured marriages for them that brought them into the upper crust of society. She tried to acquire Belisarius' immense fortune for her grandson by arranging a marriage between him and Belisarius' heiress. Another grandson, Athanasius, who was an enthusiastic apostle of the heresy of Tritheism, possessed enormous wealth and spent it freely to win converts.[17] Wealth not only gave her the luxury that she loved and allowed her to make the sort of donations to church and state that brought honor to the great families of the empire. She made an offering along with Justinian to the Arab pilgrimage shrine of Saint Sergius at Rusafa: a golden cross encrusted with gems, which was plundered by the Persian king Khusru when he raided the eastern provinces in 540.[18] She joined Justinian in restoring Antioch after the great earthquake of 525 did it such great damage that it sought emergency aid. Theodora gave the city a church dedicated to the archangel Michael and another called the basilica of Anatolius, which was built with the columns brought from Constantinople. And not only in Antioch did her donations make a statement. The crucifix set in pearls that she gave to the church in Jerusalem in 527 was splendid enough to create an impression.[19]

The Social Reformer

Theodora had hardly been crowned when she started a crusade against prostitution. It was her effort to exorcise her previous life, but it also contributed to her persona as a compassionate empress. She had known at first hand the poor women who lived a hand-to-mouth existence on the streets of the capital, selling their bodies.[20] There were more than five hundred of them plying their trade in the market outside the imperial palace, charging barely enough to live on. These were not the courtesans and dancing girls we encounter in a handful of epigrams in the *Greek Anthology*, whose lives had been relatively fortunate, though death claimed them early.[21] The women whom Theodora targeted were common prostitutes, for whom starvation was never far away. They were found in every city of the empire. There is a story of how the holy man Simeon the Fool encountered one of them who had had nothing to eat for three days until he brought her some food and wine.[22] Theodora rounded up these poor harlots from the Constantinople streets and sent them across the Bosporus to the Convent of Repentance, which she and her husband built to shelter them on the rocky shoreline. Procopius,[23] with a prurient sneer that is ill concealed, relates that some of these forcibly reformed women hated their new life so much that they hurled themselves down on the rocks, but that was in his *Secret History*. For publication he told a different story that may be closer to the truth. Brothel keepers and procurers of Constantinople were living off the earnings of poor women who were virtually their slaves. Justinian and Theodora rid the city of them and converted a palace into a convent that might serve as a refuge for women who had escaped prostitution. This "Convent of Repentance" was given an endowment and adorned with costly buildings so that none of its inmates would want to return to her old life or have to do so for financial reasons.[24] Empresses regularly endowed religious foundations to proclaim their virtue; the convent and church of Saint Euphemia where Justin and his wife were buried owed its construction to Lupicina, who had adopted the saint's name when she became empress. But a respectable woman would equally regularly keep her eyes averted from prostitutes who sold their bodies to men for a price. Theodora knew what it was like; respectable women had once avoided her in the marketplace. She endowed her convent for penitent whores not only out of compassion but perhaps defiance too.

John Malalas[25] adds details. He reports too that Theodora tried to put an end to pandering and harlotry in the capital. Sentiment against prostitution had been growing in the past century. The first Christian emperor, Constantine I, had accepted it as one of the features of urban life and had made prostitutes subject to the business tax he levied on other trades, but with the final victory of Christianity in the fifth century, the imperial government made efforts to control prostitution. Theodosius II promulgated a law prohibiting fathers from making a profit by prostituting their daughters, and the prohibition was extended to slave owners prostituting their slaves.[26] The emperor Leo banned prostitution outright and abolished the tax on it.[27] But it continued just the same. There were too many impoverished fathers with dowerless daughters, and brothel keepers toured the country villages and bought them at bargain prices. They then sold their services as prostitutes. Theodora had these whoremongers brought before her and ordered them to declare on oath what they had paid for these poor women. The average sum turned out to be five *solidi*. Theodora refunded the purchase price, freed the girls, and ordered all brothels closed. To the prostitutes she gave new clothes and a small gift of money. Malalas reports nothing of prostitutes consigned to a convent against their will. Nor does he say anything about the suicides of unhappy nuns who threw themselves over the convent walls, though Procopius' story may not be entirely untrue. Even in sixth-century Byzantium, where Saint Mary Magdalene might serve as a model, not every prostitute could have found convent life attractive.

Yet Theodora's action reflects a shallow grasp of the problem. She identified procurers and brothel keepers as the source of it, and she thought that by placing them beyond the law she would end the exploitation of poor women from indigent families. Yet the root of the problem was poverty and the dowry system, which meant that girls without dowries had little chance of making a good marriage. The brothel keepers offered an escape, and the possibility of wealth, for though most prostitutes were never far from destitution, there were exceptions. Some courtesans, like the few celebrated in the *Greek Anthology*, found generous patrons, but they were the exceptions.

By 535, in spite of Theodora's efforts, Justinian learned that prostitution was flourishing once again in the capital and procurers were going about the provinces enticing young girls, some younger than ten, by offering them fine clothes and shoes. Once in the capital they were forced to sign contracts and provide sureties; otherwise they would be kept locked up in brothels. Justinian issued a law ordering an end to prostitution and expelling the panders from Constantinople, and in its preface he wrote, "We want and pray that women may live in chastity and not be forced unwillingly into a wanton life."[28]

Where women were wronged, Theodora was ready to help. Procopius[29] remarks that it was in her nature to help unfortunate women. When Justinian's cousin Boraides died, though his wife and daughter survived him he left his property to his brother Germanus and Germanus' sons, providing only the bare legal minimum for his daughter. Justinian intervened on the daughter's behalf, to the annoyance of Germanus.[30] It was Justinian who made the intervention, but we may be sure that Theodora inspired it, all the more because it vexed Germanus and his sons, Justin and Justinian, on whom Theodora wasted no love.

There was another notorious instance too in which Theodora's intervention was unconcealed and greatly resented.[31] Artabanes was a native of Armenia and a scion of the old Armenian royal family, the Arsacids, who along with his brother commanded a contingent of Armenian troops in Africa, and when there was a mutiny there, led by the duke of Numidia, it was Artabanes and his Armenians who suppressed it. In recognition of his service, Justinian put Artabanes in command of the army in Africa. But Artabanes had fallen in love with Preïecta, the widow of the former commander in Africa whom the mutineers had murdered, and Preïecta, who was Justinian's niece, returned his affection, for Artabanes was a tall, handsome man, and she regarded him as her husband's avenger. Artabanes sent Preïecta back to Constantinople and thought up various pretexts to have himself recalled. Finally Justinian yielded. He brought Artabanes back to the capital and made him Master of the Soldiers, commander of the federate troops, and consul. His plan to marry Preïecta was progressing well. But then Theodora stepped in and aborted it.

Artabanes already had a wife in Armenia whom he had repudiated, and until his career blossomed, she had stayed quietly at home. But now that Artabanes had become a high-ranking officer, she came to Constantinople and took her case to Theodora. Theodora was sympathetic. Whatever the customs were in Armenia, under Roman law Artabanes did not have grounds to repudiate his wife. But Theodora may also have had an unspoken agenda. She saw to it that Preïecta, who was denied Artabanes, was married to the son of the old emperor Anastasius' nephew Pompeius, who had been executed for his role in the Nika riots. The family of Anastasius had provided a husband for Theodora's bastard daughter, and Preïecta's brother, Justin, the future emperor Justin II, was married to Theodora's niece, Sophia. The handsome Armenian Artabanes did not fit into Theodora's network of marriage alliances.

Artabanes had to remain wedded to his unwanted Armenian wife as long as Theodora was alive. He repudiated her as soon as Theodora was dead, but then it was too late to marry Preïecta, and his resentment led him to join a conspiracy against Justinian in late 548 or early 549. When the plot was discovered, Justinian's reaction was mild, possibly because he had a grain of sympathy for Artabanes. He was dismissed from office and kept under guard briefly within the palace, but in 550 he resumed his military career, and when we last hear of him, he was taking part in the final campaign in Italy against the Goths, which yielded victory at long last.[32]

Theodora as Builder

The buildings of Justinian advertised both his own magnificence and his compassion for his people. He built churches for the glory of God, walls and forts to preserve his subjects, and aqueducts and cisterns to provide for their well-being. In the late 550s Procopius produced a panegyric on his building program: a peculiar panegyric, for it does not follow the rhetorical rules and the literary polish is uneven, but nonetheless its purpose is clear. It intended to record and laud the structures that Justinian erected to proclaim his magnificence throughout his empire. The panegyric has little to say about Theodora, who was already dead when it was written. What it does say is flattering, but silences also carry a message. Imperial building was a sphere where Justinian preferred not to have competition that was too obvious.

So Theodora cooperated. Procopius mentions two hospices in Constantinople, the Isidorus and the Arcadius, that she built jointly with her husband.[33] He does not mention Hagia Sophia or Hagia Eirene as joint projects, both of which were rebuilt after they had been destroyed by fires in the Nika riots. But Theodora's monogram appears on their capitals, which indicates that she claimed a share of the glory. They both took credit for a new church of Saint John the Evangelist at Ephesus, for though it was finished after Theodora's death, her monogram appears on its capitals as well as Justinian's.[34] At Mount Sinai, in the church of the Theotokos in the monastery of Saint Catherine, Theodora's name appears inscribed on a beam that would originally have been visible from the ground.[35] By the time the inscription was made, Theodora was dead, but her role as Justinian's partner was still acknowledged.

When Justinian and Theodora came to the throne, Antioch was recovering from the earthquake that leveled it in May 526, and both Justinian and Theodora built churches in the reconstructed city, not jointly but as separate dedicants.[36] But as a general rule, Theodora and Justinian worked together. Yet a late tradition makes her the builder of the church of the Holy Apostles in Constantinople, which survived until it was demolished by the sultan Mehmet II to make way for the Fatih mosque.[37] The original church begun by Constantine and completed by his son, Constantius II, had fallen into disrepair and had to be reconstructed from the ground up. Procopius[38] describes the construction and assigns Theodora no role in it, and he must be right to this extent: the funds that paid for it came from the imperial treasury, not from Theodora's private fortune. But when the plans for the Holy Apostles church were drawn up, Hagia Sophia, which the Byzantines were to call simply the "Great Church," was nearing completion. Justinian had supervised its construction closely, even giving technical advice on two occasions, and it would be *his* monument, though he allowed Theodora a share of the glory. Quite possibly he turned over the supervision of the Holy Apostles project to Theodora. In 536 she laid the foundation stone.

The architects were Anthemius of Tralles, one of the team who had designed Hagia Sophia, and Isidore the Younger, who would later reconstruct Hagia Sophia's great dome after the collapse of the original one in 558. The plan must have been dictated to some extent by the plan of Constantine's church, which he built as a mausoleum for himself and his imperial successors, placing there the bones of the apostles Andrew, Luke, and Timothy to share the burial place. During Theodora's rebuilding, three wooden coffins were found in the earth under the old church. They bore inscriptions indicating that they contained the bodies of the apostles. In the two centuries after Constantine, the exact site of their interment had been forgotten.

The church was made up of two basilicas intersecting each other at right angles to form a cross. At the intersection there was a great dome supported on arches and pendentives, and over each of the arms were subsidiary domes. It was the original of the five-domed type of church, and its design was to inspire copies, such as, in Theodora's lifetime, Saint John the Evangelist in Ephesus, where the western arm of the church was lengthened to allow for two domes, and San Marco in Venice (1063–95) and in the twelfth century, Saint Front at Périgueux in southern France. At one remove is a later type, where one large dome covers the intersection and smaller domes cover side chapels. We can say little of the interior decoration of the Holy Apostles, though we know that at a later time its interior walls had a series of mosaics that showed scenes from the life of Christ on earth. They sought to educate the masses in the traditions of the church, specifically, traditions with a Chalcedonian flavor.[39] Theodora can have had nothing to do with them, but one would like to think that, except for the emphasis on Chalcedonian doctrine, she would have approved.

Legend has it that the construction of the church had a serious cost over-run. The loot taken from the Vandal kingdom provided the funds for the building, but it was not enough. Then a dream came to Theodora. The apostles Andrew, Luke, and Timothy appeared to her and told her to go to the seashore outside one of the city gates, where she would discover buried a dozen jars filled with gold. Theodora obeyed and found the jars, filled with gold pieces bearing the image of the apostles. It was enough to pay for the budget deficit. The church could be completed. Which it was, in 546, with an adjoining imperial mausoleum, where only two years later Theodora's mortal remains would be consigned to a sarcophagus of Sardian stone.

Theodora and Legal Reform

"Our most pious consort granted us by God." The words come from a law[40] promulgated in 535, a year that is crowded with reforms. Justinian acknowledges openly that he consulted his wife about a regulation that prohibited the purchase of public office. Theodora's interests were wide-ranging; in this case the problem was corruption in the bureaucracy whereby officeholders bought their offices and then sought to make profit by charging fees for their services. But there is a group of laws issued by Justinian that deal with matters that must have been closer to Theodora's heart, and although Justinian does not make any specific indication that he consulted her, we can rest assured that if he took her advice on secular simony he sought it as well on these.

A clutch of laws deal with women in the theater. Justinian acted to improve their condition. In 534 he forbade anyone to force a woman, slave or free, into the life of the theater if she was unwilling.[41] Nor could they prevent her if she chose to leave the stage. Should anyone try to stop her, the governor of the province and the bishop were to step in and prevent it. Then the law makes an interesting caveat that seems to bear the signature of Theodora, who had learned from her experience as Hecebolus' mistress. What if it is the governor of the province himself who prevents an actress from abandoning the stage? Then it is the duty of the bishop alone to vindicate the rights of the actress.

The law goes on to reiterate that former actresses, whether they are freed slaves or born free, may contract legal marriages with men of high rank and that the daughters of actresses have the same right. Theodora's footprint is visible. Two years later, another law returns to the same subject. Theater managers, it seems, were trying to control their actresses by making them swear not to leave the stage. Justinian allowed women who had sworn such an oath to break it with impunity, and for the future he prescribed a fine of ten gold pounds for anyone who exacted a promise of that sort.[42]

We can recognize Theodora's influence too in a group of laws that Justinian issued, which were intended to improve women's legal rights. She must have inspired directly or indirectly the legislation that sought to erase barriers to marriage between unequals in rank. Old Justin had already allowed a penitent former actress who had become a patrician to marry whomever she pleased, thereby opening the way for Justinian's marriage to Theodora.[43] Justinian dismantled more barriers. A free woman who had left the stage was given permission to marry even men who held *honestissimae dignitates:* that is, offices of the highest rank.[44] Daughters of actresses were granted the same right. Then a law[45] removed all prohibitions of marriage between unequals, and finally, in 541, this law was made retroactive. Even marriages contracted before the repeal of Constantine's rescript banning legal unions between unequals were to be considered legitimate.[46]

"In the service of God, there is no male nor female, nor freeman nor slave." So wrote Justinian in a law dating to 535,[47] and it was probably his respect for Theodora that led him to this view. He ruled that no woman should be put in prison, where the male guards might violate her. If she could not give bail, she should bind herself with an oath, and if she had to be detained, the detention should be in a nunnery. He vindicated the rights of women to own property and to inherit. He did not like the old custom of divorce by mutual consent and banned it, but he did recognize a list of just causes for divorce. Here, however, he was out of tune with the times, and under his successor, Justin II, divorce by mutual consent was made legal once again.

His treatment of antenuptial donations is an interesting recognition of the inequality of the sexes in marriage. Antenuptial donations were the husband's counterpart of the dowry, and in Late Antiquity it had become usual for a man to give his bride a donation before marriage just as it had long been the custom for a woman to bring a dowry to her bridegroom. Justinian ruled that the antenuptial donation should be equal in value to the dowry. A wife had to give her consent before her husband encumbered her antenuptial donation with debt, but Justinian recognized that sometimes her consent might not be entirely voluntary. He therefore ruled that she must give her consent *twice*. The law henceforth would protect her right to change her mind.

How much of this was due to Theodora? It should perhaps be noted that the one law where Justinian acknowledges his wife's input has nothing to do with the rights of women. The legal status of women had been improving slowly but steadily since the last century of the Roman Republic. Justinian did not start the trend; in fact, it is perhaps fairer to say that he marked its conclusion. We do not know what advice Theodora gave to him, except that it did not upset the status quo to any great extent. The measures that eased the social barriers for former actresses benefited her family and her old friends and thus there was self-interest involved. Theodora does not quite qualify as a modern feminist whose interest is in the status of women. Rather she was a woman acting within the Christian traditions that taught compassion for the weak and helpless and considered male and female equal in the eyes of God.

Procopius [48] relates an incident that illustrates her mind-set. Saturninus, the son of a distinguished Master of Offices, Hermogenes, who had negotiated the "Endless Peace" of 532 with Persia but was dead by this time, planned to marry the daughter of his first cousin, that is, a relation in the fourth degree, as the law measured it. Theodora snatched the bridegroom from the bridal chamber and wedded him to the daughter of an old friend from the stage, Chrysomallo. Saturninus complained to some acquaintances after the wedding night that Theodora's choice for his wife was not a virgin. No doubt she was not. When this item of gossip reached Theodora, she was incensed and had Saturninus tossed in a blanket and caned, like a schoolboy. One suspects that Procopius may not have told the whole story. But we can understand the source of Theodora's indignation. Why should men classed as *honestiores,* who had used women of the stage as prostitutes to satisfy their sexual demands, complain when they discovered that their brides were not virgins? Whatever his faults, Justinian himself was never guilty of that sort of hypocrisy.

"Then it happened that practically every woman had her character corrupted," complained Procopius.[49] "For they were all free to sin against their husbands, for such deeds brought them into no danger or hurt. Even those who were caught in adultery suffered no harm, for they went immediately to the empress and brought a counter-suit and even without laying any charge, summoned their husbands into court. What the husbands got out of it was to be made to pay back double [their wives'] dowry even though they were not found guilty, and they would be flogged and very often taken away to prison." Men lost all control of their wives, Procopius continued, and even when they were convinced that their wives were having affairs, they kept quiet. In the eyes of the upper-class beholder, what Theodora represented was revolutionary.

The Nika Revolt

The Nika uprising that erupted in Constantinople in the early days of 532 cannot be considered in isolation, for there were a number of underlying causes.[1] Street violence was a way of life, and the rough democracy of the Hippodrome provided a vehicle for popular complaints to reach the emperor. There was no equivalent of a modern police force to exercise crowd control. Before Justinian became emperor, his partisan support for the Blue party in the Hippodrome had envenomed the rivalry between the Blues and the Greens, but once he succeeded his uncle on the throne, he took firm action against the troublemakers in the cities of the empire, no matter what color they sported.[2] Yet a vivid passage in Procopius' *Secret History* gives a dissident's description of how the imperial pair still cooperated in keeping the Blues and Greens at each other's throats, which implies that their coronation may have altered their rank but not their agenda. Justinian's conversion to a law-and-order man was more apparent than real. Street violence soon reappeared; in 529 the circus had to be closed for a few months.[3] Outside the capital as well there was bloody rivalry between Blues and Greens, and the Blues got imperial protection: a governor of Cilicia was crucified for putting two Blue murderers to death.[4]

In Theodora's book, the Blues could do no wrong. Justinian appeared to be annoyed at the violence and made moves to impose law and order, but Theodora angrily defended her Blues. It was feigned anger, claimed Procopius.[5] As he saw it, the imperial partners were conniving with the aim of ruining men of property, though he goes on to remark that the Blues were more moderate than their rivals. Among the underlying causes of the Nika revolt was Theodora herself, whose pretensions must have grated Constantinople's upper crust.

Justinian remained a Blue supporter once he became emperor, and in popular perception he continued to be one all his life, even when he sought to maintain the peace.[6] There is one remarkable document that appears to be a prelude to the Nika riots that illustrates how he was perceived. The so-called *Akta dia Kalapodion*[7] records an interchange between Justinian and the Greens in the Hippodrome, and it vividly expresses the alienation of the Green party. The Greens assembled in their section of the Hippodrome and chanted a litany of complaint, and Justinian's herald replied from the imperial loge. The *Akta* appear to be an official record of the altercation, which begins on a respectful note and ends in angry invective. Somehow it was preserved. The Greens led with a protest that Calopodius[8] the *spatharius*, that is, the eunuch officer of the Attendants of the Bedchamber, was inflicting injury on them. This "Calopodius" is unknown, but the name, which means something like "Pretty Foot," may refer to a favorite of Theodora's, the eunuch Narses, who was *spatharius* during the Nika riots and played a subsidiary role in the massacre that suppressed it.

From the *Akta*, we can infer that the murder of a Green had been committed, the twenty-sixth in a series of murders. The Greens accused Justinian of responsibility, but the Blues interjected. The Greens, they said, were the only party with murderers among their number. Justinian's herald accused the Greens of blasphemy; the Blues called them detestable, and the Greens left the Hippodrome with a general curse on the audience. The *Akta* demonstrate that Justinian was still perceived as the patron and protector of the Blues, who reciprocated by supporting him. The Greens were bitter and alienated.

The two sources that take note of this dialogue date it just before the Nika riots, which broke out on Tuesday, 13 January. There had been violence in the streets, and Calopodius appears to have been the imperial officer assigned to suppress it, but he had not been impartial. The Greens chorused that they were treated as scapegoats and Justinian made no apology. The *Akta* reflect a period when the Blues perceived themselves as Justinian's allies and his favorites, as they still did in the first week of January 532, and if we are to fit the *Akta* into the calendar of events, that is where this confrontation must be dated. What may have happened is that the disgruntled Greens followed up their rejection in the Hippodrome with renewed violence, and the emperor decided to be firmer and more evenhanded. The urban prefect Eudaemon arrested a group of the rioters, both Blues and Greens, and ordered the execution of seven felons convicted of murder. Three were taken off to be hanged on the night of Saturday, 10 January. But when they were strung up, the scaffold broke. Two of the convicts, one a Blue and the other a Green, fell to the ground still alive, and monks from the nearby monastery of Saint Conon rushed out and took them into the church of Saint Lawrence for asylum. The urban prefect set a guard at the church. The Blues and Greens found a common cause.

Then, in the Hippodrome on the Ides of January (Tuesday, 13 January), the Blues and Greens, who had had the weekend to coordinate tactics, begged the emperor to show mercy to the felons in the church of Saint Lawrence, but he remained adamant. It was a confrontation similar to that described in the *Akta dia Kalopodion,* except that the two parties acted as allies. Usually twenty-four races were scheduled for one day, and the Blues and Greens continued their appeals until the twenty-second race. Then they ceased their appeals and suddenly cried in unison, "Long live the merciful Blues and Greens!" The parties, probably by prearrangement, united openly against Justinian.

Justinian beat a retreat to the Great Palace and took refuge there with his court and a group of senators. That evening the mob surged down the great main street of Constantinople, the Mese, to the Praetorium, the urban prefect's headquarters that housed the city prison. It demanded to know what the prefect was going to do about the felons in the church of Saint Lawrence. There was no answer, and the mob broke into the prison, freed the inmates, killed some guards, and set the Praetorium ablaze. Then it surged down the Mese toward the palace and set fire to the Brazen House. The flames spread across the Augustaeum, the square on which the palace faced, burned one of Constantinople's senate houses, and reached the basilica of Hagia Sophia. The conflagration destroyed it. The next day was no better. Justinian ordered races to be resumed in the Hippodrome, but the mob was beyond control. It burned the wooden seats in the Hippodrome, and the fire spread to the Baths of Zeuxippos nearby, and the baths, along with the collection of classical statues it contained, was destroyed.

The *Easter Chronicle* has a break in the manuscript where the description of the first day of the riot should be, and when it resumes someone unidentified is speaking firmly to the emperor, reproving him for failing to heed advice. Was it Theodora? The suggestion is not impossible. This critic whose name is lost faulted Justinian for his lack of firm policy, and Justinian responded by dispatching three officials[9] to ask the mob what it wanted. The mob called for the dismissal of the urban prefect, Eudaemon, the praetorian prefect, John the Cappadocian, and the *quaestor* Tribonian, the brilliant but corrupt jurist who headed the commission that was producing the great *Corpus Iuris Civilis*. They were promptly replaced, and the replacements were men who should have had the confidence of the senatorial order. Justinian knew where his support was weak. Yet the rioting did not stop.

On Thursday, 15 January, the mob raised the cry, "Another emperor for the city," and made for the palace of Probus by the Julian harbor, where they evidently hoped to find arms. Probus was a nephew of the old emperor Anastasius, and he was prudent enough to be out of town. In frustration the mob burned his palace. The arsonists went on with their work and the fires continued. One casualty that was remembered was the hospice of Samson between Hagia Eirene and Hagia Sophia. The hospice was destroyed, and the patients died in their beds.

By Saturday the situation was desperate. Loyal troops whom Justinian had summoned from Thrace arrived and attacked the rioters, but in the narrow streets of Constantinople they achieved very little. The next day, Sunday, when presumably thoughts of Christian charity might penetrate the mob mentality, Justinian entered the imperial loge bearing the Gospels, repented publicly of his errors, and offered pardon to the rioters. A few cheered, but most of the spectators yelled insults, and Justinian withdrew hurriedly. It was then, or possibly late on the previous day,[10] that Justinian made a move that could have been disastrous. He ordered many of the senators who were with him in the palace to leave and go to their homes and guard them.

This was an oddly irrational thing to do, and it is hard to fathom what Justinian had in mind. It is even more difficult to understand why he did not allow the two nephews of Anastasius, Hypatius and Pompeius, to remain behind in the palace with him. They begged the emperor to let them stay, for the mob had already tried to acclaim one nephew of Anastasius as emperor and the news of that frustrated effort must have been known inside the palace walls. But Justinian was suspicious, and the protests of the two nephews made him suspect them all the more. He could no longer count on the loyalty of the palace guards, and it could be dangerous to have potential successors so close at hand. Justinian and Theodora wanted only those people around them whom they could trust. The atmosphere within the palace was paranoid. To Procopius,[11] it seemed that the appointed destiny of Hypatius and Pompeius had at last caught up with them.

Flavius Hypatius, the eldest nephew of Anastasius, had had a long military career, although hardly a distinguished one. He was a cautious officer of only moderate ability but had never lost the confidence of the emperors he served. When his uncle died, he was in Antioch serving as Master of the Soldiers, and no one seems to have considered him seriously as Anastasius' successor. His theology seems to have been flexible; his career, begun under the pro-Monophysite Anastasius, continued under the Chalcedonian Justin I. Only in 529 did Justinian replace him as commander of the armed forces in Oriens by Belisarius.[12] Hypatius had hitherto shown no signs either of ambition or of disloyalty to Justinian, though some must have thought him open to suggestion. When the mob learned that he had been sent home from the palace, they rushed there to drag him out and make him emperor. His first reaction was terror, and his wife made a desperate effort to pull him out of the rioters' hands, but willy-nilly he was carried off to the oval forum of Constantine, nowadays marked by the stump of Constantine's column, and there the people crowned him with a gold torque. Meanwhile the senators gathered in the city's second senate house, which had escaped burning. Many of them disliked Justinian and hated Theodora, and now they shifted to what they perceived as the winning side. Hypatius had the sort of background they trusted. Justinian's expulsion of the senators from the palace had backfired. He began to consider flight.

Thus far he had retreated, attempting to conciliate the mob. It was an ineffective policy that may even have inflamed the situation. But he had little choice. The state was ill-equipped to maintain public order. Cities lacked anything like a modern police force, and in a crisis imperial officials had to turn to the army, which was trained for the battlefield, not for street fighting.[13] The troops who arrived from Thrace had failed to restore order. Fortunately there were two able commanders in the palace with Justinian, Mundo, a Gepid prince in Justinian's service, who led a corps of Herulians, and Belisarius, who had returned from the Persian front with his bodyguard of veteran soldiers. But the situation was grim. Justinian lost his nerve. He was about to load money on a fast ship and escape from the city. At this point,

Procopius, our main source for the riot, who may have been besieged in the palace himself and witnessed the incident he describes, gives Theodora a great dramatic scene that brings her vividly to life. Perhaps it possesses more poetic than historical truth, but nonetheless it is a vivid illustration of her prestige at court.[14]

Hypatius, who had been acclaimed in the Hippodrome, was at first reluctant but recovered his courage once he got word that Justinian had fled and the way was clear. The senators no longer debated whether to support the rioters. Rather the question now was how to act effectively to bring down Justinian. Procopius describes their debate with vivid imagination. Origines rose to speak. This is his sole appearance in history; and if he is not merely a literary construct, all we can say about him is that he held the rank of *illustris*, for only *illustres* could speak in the senate, but that is all we know.[15] He was the spokesman for senatorial opinion. He advised caution, pointing out that an attack on the Daphne Palace where Justinian and his court were besieged was unnecessary as well as dangerous: Hypatius could just as well be installed in some other palace in Constantinople and make it his base for the struggle. Origenes represented the sort of cautious prudence that lets zero hour pass by and loses the struggle by default. In the drama that Procopius describes, he serves as a foil for Theodora, whom the crisis stimulated to a moment of glory.

Within the Daphne Palace, the arguments went back and forth. Justinian was badly frightened. Then Theodora stood up and spoke. There is a rhetorical flavor to her speech that can hardly reproduce exactly the words she uttered, but she was an alumna of the theater and must have appreciated the drama of the moment.

As for the belief that a woman ought not show daring in the presence of men, or act boldly when men hesitate, in the present crisis, I think, we have no time left to ask if we accept it or not. For when what we hold is in extreme peril, we are left with no course of action except to make the best plan we can to deal with the plight we face. As for me, I believe that flight is not the correct course to take now, if ever, even if it serves to save our lives. For no person who has been born can escape death, but for a man who has once been emperor to become a runaway—that we cannot bear! I hope I never have the imperial purple stripped from me nor live to the day when the people I meet fail to address me as empress!

So if what you want is to save yourself, O Emperor, it's no problem. We have plenty of money; over yonder is the sea, and here are the boats. Yet ask yourself if the time will come, once you are safe, when you would gladly give up security for death. As for me, there is an ancient maxim I hold true, that says kingship makes a good burial shroud.

It was a splendid speech. This was a proud empress who had climbed from the dregs of society to the peak of the social order, and she would die rather than slide down the ladder again. She would be *despoinis* and *basilissa* or she would be nothing! If the choice was between slaughtering the mob or laying aside the purple, she was for slaughter. To be sure, the proverb she quotes is not quite right, and Procopius may himself have made the emendation with concealed irony. The old maxim said that *tyranny* made a good winding sheet,[16] and "tyranny" was very different from "kingship." But it would never do to call Justinian's regime a tyranny, although massacring one's enemies was the mark of a tyrant rather than a true king.

In any case, whatever words Theodora may actually have used in the moment of crisis, she rallied the beleaguered cadre of loyalists. Belisarius with the battle-hardened veterans of his guard and Mundo with his corps of barbarian Herulians attacked the mob that had gathered in the Hippodrome to acclaim Hypatius. The Blue and Green alliance was already beginning to crack, for the eunuch Narses, one of the ablest tacticians the empire was to produce, had been judiciously distributing bribes. But it was the massacre in the Hippodrome that saved the regime. It was ruthless and bloody, and it worked. Some thirty-five thousand were killed.

Hypatius and Pompeius were seized as they gazed down on the bloodbath from the imperial loge, and they were brought before the emperor who found their protestations unconvincing. He condemned them to death. Hypatius made a pitiful attempt at a defense: he claimed he had brought the mob to the Hippodrome so that Justinian could massacre them, but Justinian, with some sarcasm, asked why he had waited to do it until half the city was burned. By Tuesday, 20 January, exactly a week after the riot began, a stunned quiet pervaded the city. People stayed off the streets and only a few shops selling food staples were open. It was several days before the markets returned to normal.

Our chief account of the riot comes from Procopius, who recognized the key role Theodora's courage played, even though he did not like her. Other accounts add details. Count Marcellinus, who was adding a sequel to his Latin chronicle at this time and writes as a contemporary, claims that Anastasius' nephews, Hypatius, Pompeius, and Probus, were the ringleaders,[17] and there was a legend that got as far west as the land of the Franks that the revolt was a protest against Theodora whose mere presence in the palace marked a social revolution and offended the old elite.[18] From the eastern provinces there is the Syriac *Chronicle* of Zachariah of Mytilene, which blames John the Cappadocian, the praetorian prefect.[19] He had been appointed to his office less than a year before, but he had set about reforms with alarming vigor, and in Constantinople people were loud with their complaints and wanted John dismissed. Their outcries were constant, reports the *Chronicle*, and violence escalated to the point that the workshops were closed and the palace doors shut. The Blues and Greens gathered in the Hippodrome and made Hypatius emperor. Mundo was the general who led the slaughter in the Hippodrome; Belisarius is not mentioned. Distance from Constantinople has exaggerated the number of victims; "Zachariah"[20] puts it at more than eighty thousand. He also reported that when Anastasius' nephews were brought before Justinian, he would have spared them had it not been for Theodora. "His [Justinian's] consort grew angry, and swore by God and by him, and also adjured him to have the men put to death. And they were sent to the seashore and killed and thrown into the sea." Theodora may have sought to display a compassionate public image, but let anyone threaten her grasp on power and she could be merciless. In the Nika revolt she showed her steely side. Justinian must have regarded her thereafter with new respect. He himself was more inclined to leniency; he pardoned Hypatius posthumously and no doubt Pompeius too and restored their property to their children.[21]

Theodora's Friends and Enemies

It was never prudent to get in Theodora's way, for if she was a reliable friend and stouthearted ally, she was also a ruthless adversary who was alert to any threat. After she met Justinian and married him, she put her past life behind her and guarded her reputation carefully, for Justinian valued chastity in women. "It is Our wish that everyone lead chaste lives, so far as is possible," he wrote in one of his laws,[1] and Theodora lived up to his code. The one factor that could have driven a wedge between him and Theodora was a well-founded rumor that she was unfaithful and had taken a lover. On that score, she was careful. When scandal arose connecting her with a courtier named Areobindus, a young, handsome barbarian whom Theodora had appointed to her staff, she swiftly nipped it in the bud. She first made a point of treating Areobindus badly and then he disappeared from court. No one heard of him again.[2] The romance of Theodora and Areobindus was eventually to become a vehicle for the great actress, Sarah Bernhardt, but the historical record has nothing more to tell about him.

Procopius also reports the fate of Priscus, Count of the Excubitors and an ex-consul, and it is instructive. Theodora had her own network of agents who kept her informed of the rumors in the marketplace, and what she heard of Priscus was unsettling. He was corrupt, rapacious, and wealthy, and, even worse, he saw to it that disparaging scuttlebutt about her reached Justinian's ears. But she found him hard to remove, for Justinian was easygoing and reluctant to dismiss officials so long as they performed their duties adequately. But finally Theodora won over her husband. Priscus was bundled off in midwinter across the Sea of Marmora and put into prison at Cyzicus. But he tunneled out of his cell, fled to sanctuary, and ended his life as a cleric.

Procopius' report makes Theodora alone responsible for Priscus' fall from grace. She had him seized, hustled onboard ship, and sent to a location she had chosen herself. He was taken in his sanctuary, his head was shaven, and an involuntary ordination catapulted him into the priesthood. Justinian averted his eyes, though Procopius notes that he confiscated Priscus' property nonetheless. But another source makes Justinian the coauthor of the deed: it was Justinian himself who ordered Priscus made a deacon.[3]

Germanus, Justinian's cousin, was a particular target for her malice, and she made no secret of it. Like Justinian, Germanus was a nephew of old Justin, and once he became emperor, he made him commander of the army in Thrace, replacing Vitalian. It was a sensitive posting and Germanus handled it well. Unlike Justinian who never led an army on campaign, Germanus was a brilliant field commander, and as soon as he was appointed Master of the Troops in Thrace, he showed his ability by inflicting a stunning defeat on a horde of Bulgar and Slav invaders who had crossed the Danube and penetrated as far south as the pass of Thermopylae.[4] By 519 he had become a senator with the rank of *illustris,* which gave him the right to speak in the senate. To an outsider comparing Justin's two nephews, Germanus must have seemed the more promising.

Outwardly, at least, Justinian seemed unworried, but Theodora took note. Germanus' career stalled while Justinian's moved forward. Yet it was he whom Justinian picked to suppress a revolt in Africa in 536, when the army mutinied and its commander, Solomon, had to flee to Sicily to seek help from Belisarius. Germanus restored peace in Africa and then, three years later, was replaced. In 540, when the shah of Persia, Khusru, breached the Endless Peace of 532 and invaded the eastern provinces, Germanus was sent with only three hundred troops to defend Antioch. It was an impossible task, and the best Germanus could do was to get out of Khusru's way. Antioch fell, and Germanus was denied a victory.

Yet if Justinian were to die, Germanus was his obvious heir, and as long as Theodora hoped to bear a son, she regarded him as a threat. Even after she had abandoned hope of a child, she considered him no friend to herself, and certainly not to her family, whom she had raised up from the gutter. As long as she lived, she blocked any advancement for Germanus and his sons. But Germanus seems not to have been overly anxious for high office. He waited, patiently enough but surely with concealed resentment. It was only after Theodora's death that Justinian gave him a major command that fitted his talents. Then, after some hesitation, he placed him in charge of the Gothic War in Italy, which was going badly.

Germanus evidently intended to win over the Goths by nurturing a pro-Byzantine "Fifth Column" among them, for his preparations included marrying the granddaughter of Theodoric, Matasuintha, and getting her pregnant. His plan may have been to rebuild Italy by uniting the Goths and the Byzantines under a revived dynasty descended both from the great Theodoric the Amal and the house of Justinian. But his chance came too late. He died in the early autumn 550, before he could reach Italy. A son by Matasuintha was born posthumously, but he made no mark in history. Germanus' sons by his previous marriage, Justin and Justinian, inherited his military talent, and if ability had been the sole criterion, Justin would have succeeded Justinian when he died in 565. But the legacy of Theodora's malice helped to shape the choice, and the next emperor was another Justin, the husband of her niece, Sophia.

One consequence of Theodora's hostility was that Germanus could find no marriage partners for his children. His sons remained unwed until near middle age, and his daughter Justina reached eighteen with no husband in sight. Then John, Vitalian's nephew, arrived in Constantinople, fresh from the Gothic War in Italy. His uncle's reputation clouded his prospects, but he was an able officer and prepared to wed Justina. This was a marriage above his station, and Germanus would have preferred a son-in-law of higher rank, but no other suitor was ready to brave Theodora's wrath. And wrathful she was: when she failed to break the engagement, she threatened to destroy John, and as a result, she damaged Byzantine fortunes in the Gothic War. For when John returned to Italy, he feared that the empress had sent instructions to her friend, Antonina, to dispose of him, and he knew Antonina's reputation as an able, ruthless woman. Hence he was careful to keep his distance from her.

But Antonina's husband, Belisarius, was John's commander, and when Belisarius went to war, his wife went with him. John had little respect for Belisarius in any case, but fear of Antonina added to his distrust. The atmosphere among Belisarius' general staff in Italy grew more poisonous, and their lack of cooperation contributed to the failure of the campaign. The war against the Ostrogoths dragged on, and the suffering and the cost escalated. So Procopius[5] reports, exaggerating the truth. But palace politics were fertile soil for paranoia, and Procopius' story has some ring of truth.

With Antonina herself, Theodora had an uneven relationship, but the bond between them was durable enough that Belisarius used his wife as a go-between. We do not know how the two women met; perhaps Theodora recruited her as an agent and an informer from the demimonde of the theater and rapidly learned to appreciate her ability. The two women had similar backgrounds: Antonina's father and grandfather had been charioteers, and her mother had been one of the despised strippers who displayed their charms in theater orchestras. She was no longer young when she married Belisarius, and there were rumors that she had had several children: one, a son named Photius, was to leave a mark in history, albeit a black one, by suppressing a Samaritan revolt with utmost cruelty,[6] and there was a daughter as well, who was wooed by an officer of slight competence, Sergius, who thus earned himself Theodora's favor.[7]

The same law of Justin I[8] that removed the legal obstacles to the marriage of Justinian and Theodora smoothed the way for Antonina's marriage to the young guardsman, Belisarius. Possibly it was Theodora who first introduced her to this ambitious young trooper and promoted his rapid rise to a command post. Belisarius was devoted to his wife, and though she was unfaithful, she was circumspect, not because she was afraid of her husband, but because she feared the empress' new recognition of the chaste wedlock. Whatever Theodora's youth had been, she was now a convert to marital fidelity. Yet Antonina was Belisarius' steady supporter and helpmate. She accompanied him on his campaigns in Africa and Italy. On the voyage of the expedition to Africa, it was she who prevented the water on Belisarius' flagship from going bad by storing it in glass jars embedded in sand to prevent breakage and kept in the dark to check the growth of algae. When the Goths subjected Rome to a terrible siege for a year and nine days in 537–38, she was the envoy whom Belisarius sent to Naples to organize a shipment of grain for the beleaguered city.[9] Theodora used her as her agent to depose Pope Silverius and clear the way for a successor who promised to be more pliable.[10] Antonina carried out her mission for Theodora with ruthless efficiency. Silverius was accused of treason and whisked off the papal throne into exile with breathtaking speed.

Yet there were undertones to the relationship between the empress and Antonina that were less amiable. Theodora was anxious to marry her grandson to Belisarius' only child, Joannina, who would inherit her father's immense fortune. The betrothal[11] was made when Belisarius' fortunes were parlous: Justinian fell ill with the plague that ravaged Constantinople in 542, and in the midst of this crisis, when the death of Theodora's partner could have finished her ascendancy then and there, she learned that Belisarius, field marshal of the army in the East, and a fellow officer, Bouzes, had anticipated events and were discussing the succession. It was reported that they stated they would never accept another emperor like Justinian.

The incident shows how decisively and ruthlessly Theodora could act when her power was threatened. All her authority was derived from her husband, and if he were to die, the best she could do to preserve some part of it was to influence the succession. Thus when two officers belonging to the general staff tattled and informed Theodora that there was talk in headquarters about what would happen if Justinian were to die, she summoned the commanders and investigated. Bouzes was called into the women's quarters in the palace, and when he came, unsuspecting and thinking Theodora had some private message for him, he was thrown into an underground apartment and stayed there in solitary confinement for two years and four months. Then Theodora let him resume his military career, but his eyesight never recovered from his ordeal.[12]

As for Belisarius, who had also talked imprudently about Justinian's successor, he was relieved of his command at Theodora's insistence and remained under suspicion, in fear for his life, until Justinian reappointed him in 544 to command the war against the Ostrogoths. He was in no position at this point in his career to oppose the betrothal, nor was Antonina. But once in Italy, Antonina kept postponing the wedding until Theodora grew suspicious. So, feeling that her life was nearing its end, she arranged to have Joannina and Anastasius live together as lovers, unmarried, which would compromise the girl indelibly unless a wedding followed. Yet Theodora's misgivings were well-founded, for as soon as she died, Antonina ended the engagement. Joannina and Anastasius had by then lived together for eight months and had fallen deeply in love, but neither her daughter's feelings nor any regard for the dead empress deflected Antonina's purpose.[13]

It was Antonina's affair with a handsome young Thracian named Theodosius that allowed Theodora to bind Antonina to her. We do not know why Belisarius adopted Theodosius, except that he may have wanted to further the career of a fellow Thracian. He performed the adoption ceremony on the eve of his African campaign, though apparently not legally, for Theodosius did not become his heir. Antonina soon lusted after the young Thracian, and the affair blossomed during the African campaign and carried over into the Gothic War, and though it became common knowledge among Belisarius' staff, he could believe no ill of his wife. Finally a slave girl tattled, and Belisarius, mad with jealousy, ordered Theodosius killed. But Theodosius was warned in time and fled to Ephesus. Antonina managed to soothe Belisarius' suspicions and even persuaded him to let her punish the tattling slave, which she did with utmost cruelty.

Yet Theodosius would not return to Antonina, for he was afraid of her son, Photius, who identified with his stepfather, Belisarius, and regarded his own mother with the disgust and antipathy of a rejected child. So Antonina engineered an assignment for Photius in Constantinople, and Theodosius came back to Antonina's embraces for as long as she was in Italy. After the surrender of Ravenna in 540, he returned with her to Constantinople. But he was an unhappy lover, a little frightened by Antonina's passion, and he once again left her and retired to Ephesus where he became a monk. Antonina's distress was such that even her naive, cuckolded husband was persuaded to ask Justinian to recall Theodosius. But as long as Belisarius was in the capital, Theodosius stayed away.

However, in 541 Belisarius was dispatched to the eastern front, and Antonina remained behind briefly to help Theodora bring down the praetorian prefect, John the Cappadocian, and also to enjoy Theodosius. Yet Photius was still a potential liability who could expose her. Antonina tried to drive a wedge between him and Belisarius. But Photius realized that his mother was vilifying him to her husband and saw to it that Belisarius discovered what was going on in Constantinople between Antonina and Theodosius. Belisarius was overwhelmed and distraught, and he and Photius swore an oath together to take vengeance on Theodosius. Meanwhile Antonina, who had ensnared John the Cappadocian for Theodora and thus earned her gratitude, set out to the eastern front to join her husband, who received her coldly. Theodosius left Constantinople and returned to Ephesus. There Photius arrested him. Theodosius sought asylum in the church of Saint John, but the bishop took a bribe and gave him up to Photius. Theodosius was taken off to a secret hideaway. He disappeared.

At this point Theodora took a hand. First she subjected some comrades of Belisarius and Photius to tough interrogation, and then she had Photius himself flogged, but they would not reveal where Theodosius was confined. However, the secret could not be kept.[14] Theodora discovered the hideaway and had Theodosius brought to Constantinople, where she presented him as an unexpected gift to an overjoyed Antonina. Belisarius was soon brought to heel. Justinian had recovered from the plague, and he was not amused to learn that his renowned general had been discussing the succession. Theodora waited until Belisarius was contrite and thoroughly frightened before she moved to reassure him, letting him know that she was acting out of regard for Antonina. As for Theodosius, Theodora kept him in the palace and showered favors on him, even pledging to make him a general in the army. His future as Theodora's favorite seemed auspicious. However, an attack of dysentery killed him before Theodora could make good her promises.

Theodora's most rancorous animosity was directed against John the Cappadocian. John was an uncultured man with no respect for the traditions of the praetorian prefect's office, and he was rumored to be a secret pagan, but that was probably hostile gossip, for a charge of paganism, if proved, would have ended his career. Yet he was an efficient tax collector, and Justinian valued his services. He had been forced to sacrifice him during the Nika revolt in January 532. But by 18 October of the same year he was back in office, and in the latter half of the decade he undertook a reform program to reduce bureaucratic waste, thereby making a host of enemies, for the bureaucracy was the educated elite's road to wealth. For Byzantium's equivalent of the chattering classes, John was an ogre.

Yet when John spoke, Justinian heeded. He listened to John when he counseled against sending an expedition against the Vandal kingdom in 533 and would have canceled it except that a bishop from the East arrived at court and disclosed that he had had a dream that instructed him to rebuke the emperor for failing to support the Catholics in Africa against their Vandal persecutors. John was outspoken and fearless, and he did not hesitate to denounce Theodora to Justinian. He almost succeeded in creating a rift between her and her husband. As if that were not enough, he supported the Greens and Theodora was a devoted Blue.[15]

We have two reports of John the Cappadocian's fall. Both point to Theodora as its author. One relates simply that the empress, who was vigilant to prevent injustice, approached Justinian with a full account of John's villainy, which had thus far escaped the emperor's notice. But even after Theodora's warning, Justinian was uncertain what to do, for John had made himself necessary, and Justinian could not bring himself to dismiss him. Other officials gave him a wide berth.[16] The other account, from Procopius, is full of the cut and thrust of court intrigue and tells how Theodora got rid of a potentate whose power had become so great that it threatened the regime.[17]

By 540 John's power was at its height. He had a huge bodyguard and lived in a luxurious new palace where he entertained lavishly and wallowed in debauchery. In the bowels of his official residence he built a dungeon where he had people tortured and even killed to part them from their money. Theodora sensed the danger and was determined to bring him down. Procopius does not mention her futile effort to get Justinian to act. Instead he tells how she enlisted Antonina's help. Antonina had her own agenda, for she knew that if she did Theodora a favor, she could expect one in return. She set a trap and baited it shrewdly. She insinuated herself into the confidence of John's only child, Euphemia, and talked openly with her. She revealed that her husband, Belisarius, was unhappy. He had just returned, victorious, from Italy, and though the victory would turn out to be hollow, that was not yet apparent. Yet the welcome he had received from Justinian was cool. He was not granted another triumph, and he was bitter. Antonina made a point of letting Euphemia know how disaffected he was. With her father as an ally, Antonina intimated, Belisarius could topple Justinian. If Justinian were gone, Belisarius and John would both benefit. Euphemia was receptive. She knew that this was news that her father would like to hear, and she reported her conversation to him.

It is not clear why John rose to the bait, for he detested Belisarius. It may be that he hoped to entangle him in a plot and discredit him. Or perhaps his ambition blinded him. It may have been out of a mixture of motives, including simple opportunism, that he agreed to meet Antonina in a villa that Belisarius owned in the suburb of Rufinianae. Theodora, whom Antonina had kept informed, saw to it that two trusted officers were concealed at the meeting place: the eunuch Narses who was later to conquer the Ostrogoths in Italy, and the Count of the Excubitors, Marcellus. She passed on word of the snare to Justinian, and there was a rumor that Justinian sent a veiled hint to John to avoid the rendezvous. The rumor cannot have been true. But it was in character for Justinian to waver, just as it was in character for Theodora to act boldly.

John did not scent the danger, as he would have done if he had guessed from the rumored hint that Justinian had foreknowledge of the rendezvous. But he arrived with a corps of bodyguards who always attended him, for he feared assassination. He and Antonina talked, and Narses and Marcellus overheard him agreeing to her seditious proposals. They rushed out to arrest him, but the bodyguards intervened, Marcellus was wounded, and John fled. Had he gone to Justinian without delay and revealed the whole story, he might have saved himself, Procopius thought, but he lost his nerve. He took refuge in a church.

He was banished to a suburb of Cyzicus on the Asian side of the Sea of Marmara and ordained a deacon. Yet he refused to perform any clerical duties for he still hoped for a comeback. But when a youth gang killed the unpopular bishop of Cyzicus, John fell under suspicion, for it was known there was no love lost between him and the victim. No evidence connected him with the murder, but he was punished just the same. He was flogged, stripped of his property, and banished to Egypt. His palace in Constantinople was granted to Belisarius. Yet Theodora was not satisfied; even in Egypt she pursued him and tried to have him convicted of the bishop's murder. Not until after Theodora's death did Justinian recall him, and by then time had passed him by. He could not resume his career in the bureaucracy.

His successor as prefect did not last long; Procopius claimed he was not corrupt enough for Justinian and Theodora, though he was no paragon. Then Theodora found a man with the qualifications she liked: a Syrian banker named Peter Barsymes (Bar-Simon).[18] He knew how to raise money. He cheated the soldiers of their pay, or so Procopius claimed with great indignation. Frontier militia (*limitanei*) had their pay canceled, and the wages for the field soldiers were delayed. He sold offices, ignoring Justinian's law of 535[19] that had banned the practice. These were years of financial desperation following the epidemic of plague, and revenues were more important than scruples.

Barsymes also tried to make a profit for the treasury by grain speculation: one year when there was a surplus stored in the state granaries, he forced the cities in the East to buy it, even though it had begun to rot and was no longer fit to eat. They had to dump it, which left them with not enough to feed themselves. But the grain harvest in Egypt was still abundant, and so Barsymes emptied the state granaries by selling these cities what was not needed for Constantinople, gambling that the next year's harvest would be as bountiful as before. It was not. Faced with a grain shortage in the capital, Barsymes made compulsory purchases in Bithynia, Phrygia, and Thrace. Transport overland was necessary, an enormously expensive enterprise compared with water transport that was used for grain from Egypt, but Barsymes dealt with this difficulty by assigning transportation costs to the provinces that had to supply the grain.

Yet Constantinople needed still more. The outcry the shortfall caused, added to the protests of the soldiers who did not receive their pay, was enough to turn Justinian against Barsymes. But Theodora continued to defend him. Nonetheless, Justinian dismissed him on 1 May 546. Theodora's influence had limits. Barsymes had held the office for three years less two and a half months.

However, Barsymes was still Theodora's favorite. She admired his competence, and the next year she got him an appointment as Count of the Sacred Largesses, overseeing imperial revenues and expenses. He continued to find novel ways to raise money, enriching himself in the process, but that was condoned by the ethics of the bureaucracy. Procopius claimed that he had lightweight gold *solidi* minted, and lightweight gold coins have been found, which gives credence to the charge. Probably they were intended to defray some charge against the treasury, perhaps civil service salaries. The need for coinage was enormous, for until the plague year, 542, the imperial economy was expanding, driven by conquest. There were twice as many mints at work producing coins in Justinian's reign as in old Justin's time.[20]

Barsymes also turned the silk trade into a source of wealth both for the treasury and for himself. Silk came to the Mediterranean from China, either by sea via Sri Lanka, where it was bought by Persian traders who carried it into the empire, or by land through the steppes of Central Asia. The cities of Beirut and Tyre had an ancient reputation for silk weaving. Silk was the fabric of choice for church vestments and the garments that courtiers wore, and the prices of raw silk went up. The silk merchants blamed the Persian middlemen and the tariffs the silk traders had to pay at the imperial customshouses. Justinian put a ceiling on the price: eight gold *solidi* for one pound of silk. The result was a black market.

Then Theodora took a hand. She seized the silk cargoes, and Barsymes set up a silk monopoly: henceforth the silk weavers were to work for the Sacred Largesses office, and silk dye was sold publicly in the marketplace. The trade was centralized, private importers were squeezed out, and the silk workers in cities that had once prospered from the trade were unemployed; many emigrated to Persia. Thus, wrote Procopius, Barsymes made great profits for the emperor and still more for himself.[21] He survived Theodora's death; Justinian appointed him praetorian prefect again in 555 and he lasted seven years in the office, which cannot be taken as evidence of good behavior, for Justinian in his old age was notoriously reluctant to bring in new blood. In 562 a street gang of Blues set fire to Barsymes' house, which was not a mark of popularity. But he built a splendid palace to replace it, which became imperial property after his death.

We cannot whitewash Theodora's record. Germanus was as able a military leader as Belisarius, but Theodora kept him sidelined. John the Cappadocian was corrupt, but the standards of the day judged self-enrichment in high office leniently. Theodora brought him down because she perceived him as a threat. The administration of Barsymes was no great improvement compared to John's, but he lacked the independent power base that John had built up. He was Theodora's man. Her consistent policy was to protect both her husband's position and her own, and since her power was dependent on her husband's, she betrayed a sense of insecurity that Justinian himself did not feel. Justinian did not consider Germanus a serious threat, he appreciated John the Cappadocian's efficiency, and, in general, he was inclined to treat the misdemeanors of his underlings leniently.

The *Secret History*'s recital of the implacable rancor with which Theodora hunted down her enemies is devastating judgment. It portrays an empress whose real character was actually the opposite of the reputation she cultivated: not merciful and compassionate but ruthless and paranoid. She had a mind-set, claimed the *Secret History,* that was utterly inhumane. Nothing could persuade her to abandon a grudge or forgive an enemy. "No one ever saw Theodora become reconciled with a man who had offended her, not even after he was dead. Instead the son of the dead man inherited the empress' hatred up to the third generation like any other legacy that was passed on from his father."[22]

We cannot accept the *Secret History* at face value. But it reflects the reputation that Theodora had in the ruling circles of Constantinople. Overstated it may be, but this much is clear: no one incurred Theodora's enmity willingly, or failed to regret it if he did.

Theodora and Foreign Policy

Five forty-two was the year bubonic plague first reached Europe. It had appeared the year before in Egypt, where it devastated Alexandria, and then it moved up the east coast of the Mediterranean to Palestine. People told tales of how they saw boats of bronze traveling swiftly across the sea, rowed by boatmen without heads. Reports of the epidemic reached the capital. It made its way inexorably through Syria and the provinces of Asia Minor, emptying villages except for a handful of survivors who were left to cope with the great mass of corpses. Crops could not be harvested for lack of farm laborers, and livestock was left untended.

Then the plague reached Constantinople, and first it attacked the poor and homeless who lived in the streets. John of Ephesus reported that the dead taken from the city were counted until the number reached 230,000, and then the enumerators at the city gates and the harbors stopped counting.[1] Justinian appointed a referendary named Theodore for the relief of the sick and the dead. The tombs were soon filled, and the grave diggers who were digging trenches for communal graves could not keep up with the number of corpses. So they were taken across the Golden Horn and thrown down into the fortification towers along the walls of Sycae, modern Galata. There they rotted, and their stench befouled the city.[2]

Then Justinian himself fell ill, and it must have been Theodora who provided what governmental direction there was. She cannot have known if or when her husband's death would set off a power struggle she might not survive. Imperial prestige had slumped in the eastern provinces. Not only was there the plague, but renewed war as well. The Persians reopened the war in 540 and the Byzantines were caught unprepared. Antioch was taken and destroyed. Luckily, the year before the plague reached the capital, Theodora had brought down her enemy, John the Cappadocian, who would have grabbed power if he were able. But he was safely in exile.

It was a grim period. The plague was a turning point in the fortunes of the empire. The men and women dying on the streets must have seemed a manifestation of the wrath of God who was displeased with his people, and it is no coincidence that during the plague year Justinian dispatched a missionary to the provinces of Asia, Lydia, Caria, and Phrygia to wipe out pagan survivals there and terminate the heresy of Montanism. The Montanists in Phrygia did not abandon their faith without a struggle. Many shut themselves up in their churches and set them on fire rather than yield. The missionary chosen for this assignment was a friend of Theodora, John of Ephesus, who reports that he made seventy thousand converts, destroyed pagan temples, and founded ninety-six churches and twelve monasteries.[3] John, who was a convinced Monophysite, was probably Theodora's choice. The fall of John the Cappadocian left her no rival as Justinian's adviser.

She said as much in a letter that she sent about this time to a Persian nobleman named Zaberganes whom she had recently met when he came on a diplomatic mission to Constantinople. The date of his visit may have been just after the sack of Antioch, for he had been one of the Persian commanders there; he was the lieutenant who urged the Persian king to push home the assault and massacre the Antiochenes.[4] It was a well-crafted letter: Theodora greeted Zaberganes as one whom she knew as a person of goodwill, and she urged him to persuade his king to make peace, promising unspecified benefits if he succeeded. If the letter had fallen into the wrong hands, it might have compromised Zaberganes. But he was no fool. He himself gave the letter to Khusru, who read it, and its last sentence made an impression on him. Theodora could promise Zaberganes rewards because, she claimed, Justinian did nothing without consulting her.[5]

We know about this letter because Khusru used it to his advantage in 543. The plague that ravaged Constantinople had not spared Persia. Khusru's army had suffered heavy losses campaigning in Lazica in the mountainous country south of the Black Sea, and his son had rebelled. The Persian notables were disenchanted with him. To counter the disaffection, Khusru read them Theodora's letter aloud and asked what sort of state they thought it was where a woman was in charge. Male chauvinists to a man, the notables were shocked, which, we are told, somehow allayed their dissatisfaction with their own king.

The author of the story is Procopius, who was no friend of feminine power and thought Theodora's authority in state affairs diminished imperial prestige in Persian eyes.[6] Procopius is not an impartial witness; he disapproved of Theodora's meddling in foreign affairs. Yet Theodora's private letter merely complemented Justinian's official efforts. The empire needed peace. Theodora clearly had made a point of trying to strike up a friendship with Zaberganes when he visited Constantinople, and now she tried to make him her lobbyist at the Persian court, or if she failed in that, to compromise him. She succeeded in neither aim, and—unexpectedly—Khusru turned the letter to his own advantage. But it was a clever ploy.

About the same time, Theodora made a bold move to win over the Nobadae south of the First Cataract of the Nile for the Monophysites. A few years earlier, in 537, the duke of the Thebaid on Justinian's orders had closed down the shrine of Isis at Philae and handed over Isis' temple to the local bishop. The Nobadae were ripe for conversion. Monophysite fortunes had not been faring well. In 537 the Monophysite patriarch of Alexandria, Theodosius, whom Theodora supported, was brought to Constantinople where he was to remain until his death, and Justinian appointed a Chalcedonian to replace him. In Alexandria, Theodosius had been beleaguered by radical Monophysites variously known as Aphthartodocetists, Julianists, or Gaianists, who carried the One-Nature doctrine to its extreme, but in exile he became the acknowledged leader of mainstream Monophysitism. From his refuge in Constantinople, which Theodora provided, he watched over the fortunes of the Monophysites as best he could. In 541 the Chalcedonians had the upper hand.

Perhaps the plague that smote Egypt in 541, a year before it reached Constantinople, concentrated men's minds and made Theodora into a bolder apostle of the Monophysites. Our authority for how Christianity came to the pagan Nobadae of northern Nubia comes from John of Ephesus, who relates that in that year a presbyter named Julian, one of the Monophysite exiles in Constantinople attached to Theodosius, asked Theodora to send him as a missionary to the Nobadae. Theodora was delighted, but she consulted her husband. She may well have anticipated no serious objection. Monophysites and Chalcedonians were united in their horror of paganism. But Justinian did not want a Monophysite church to the south of Egypt, for at this point he was trying to establish a Melkite patriarchate in Alexandria to challenge the anti-Chalcedonians on their home turf. He dispatched his own mission, equipped with gold and baptismal robes, and sent orders to the duke of the Thebaid to help it on its way.

John of Ephesus describes Theodora's counteraction:

> When the queen learned these things, she quickly, with much cunning, wrote letters to the duke of the Thebaid, and sent a mandatory of her court to carry them to him, which were as follows: "Inasmuch as both his majesty and myself have decided to send an embassy to the Nobadae, I am now dispatching a blessed man named Julian; and it is, moreover, my will that my ambassador reach the aforesaid people before his majesty's. Be warned that if you permit his ambassador to arrive there before mine, and do not hinder him by various pretexts until mine shall have reached you, and passed through your province and arrived at his destination, your life shall answer for it, for I will immediately send and take off your head."[7]

The duke took Theodora's threat seriously. He valued his head and considered it more prudent to incur Justinian's wrath than Theodora's. When Justinian's envoy with his party reached him, he delayed them with the excuse that he had to find pack animals, but when Julian and his party arrived, guides and horses were ready. Then the duke reported to Justinian's envoy that Theodora's mission had seized the animals he had collected for them and had departed. "And I am too well acquainted with the fear in which the queen is held to dare to stand in their way," he said.

The emperor's envoy was angry and made terrible threats, but he could only wait while fresh guides and horses were prepared, and when at last he reached Silko, the king of the Nobadae, he found that Julian had completed his conversion of the royal court. The reception that Silko gave the emperor's envoy followed Julian's instructions. The king accepted Justinian's presents and sent gifts in return, but, he said, "his [Justinian's] faith we cannot accept, for if we consent to become Christians, we shall walk after the example of the patriarch Theodosius." They would not abandon their paganism for "the wicked faith professed by the emperor." Julian continued his mission in the northern Nubian kingdom for two years, though he suffered terribly from the hot climate, and then he returned to Constantinople where Theodora welcomed him back.[8]

Julian converted the royal court of Nobatia, but it is not clear how successful he was among the general population. After his departure, the bishop of Philae continued a missionary program in Nobatia until 551, and then there was a hiatus until long after Theodora's death. In 569 the patriarch Theodosius consecrated another Monophysite missionary, Longinus, and sent him to the Nobadae, and it was he who completed the conversion.

The story of how Christianity reached the Nobadae has two points of interest. First, it describes a rare occasion when Theodora undertook to thwart Justinian, and when the duke of the Thebaid had to choose between arousing Justinian's wrath or Theodora's, he recognized that Theodora was the more ruthless of the two and appeased her. All this happened while the plague was raging, and Justinian needed Theodora, which helps to explain his mild reaction. He did not attempt to countermand her orders or interfere with her mission's progress, for he—and Justin before him—championed Christianity over paganism outside the borders of the empire, disregarding differences in dogma.[9] Second, imperial foreign policy in northern Nubia was served quite as well by Theodora as it would have been by Justinian. The Nobadae, once converted, were willing to follow Justinian's orders and control the Blemmyes, who were nomadic raiders preying on the villagers of upper Egypt and slaying isolated hermits. Theodora's and Justinian's policies might diverge, but neither lost sight of the general good of the empire.

When bold action was needed, Theodora was prepared. Procopius accused her in the *Secret History* of plotting the murder of Amalasuintha, the daughter of Theodoric the Ostrogoth,[10] for she sensed that this wellborn, accomplished woman would be a rival if she sought refuge in Justinian's court. She was apprehensive of her husband's inconstancy, not so much that he might be unfaithful to her bed, as that he might turn to Amalasuintha for advice. The tale goes like this: at Theodora's urging, Justinian sent a protégé of hers, Peter the Patrician, to carry on negotiations with the king of the Ostrogoths, Theodahad. Theodahad was Amalasuintha's cousin, whom she had brought to the throne after her son Athalaric ended his short life of debauchery by dying of a wasting disease. She imagined that she could dominate him, even though there had never been any love lost between the two. Theodahad had a reputation as a student of philosophy, which was unusual for a Goth, and Amalasuintha, who was more than half assimilated to classical culture herself, may have thought that a philosopher could not be a bad king. She was soon disabused of that notion. Theodahad deposed her and threw her into prison.

The story that Procopius tells in his *Wars of Justinian*[11] reports that Peter was dispatched to Italy ostensibly to negotiate about Lilybaeum (Marsala) in Sicily, which Justinian claimed, for it had belonged to the Vandal kingdom that had surrendered to him. But he was also instructed to negotiate secretly with Amalasuintha, who had already sent feelers to Justinian earlier, to seek help when she realized that her son's death was imminent. Peter's orders were also to have secret talks with Theodahad about Tuscany, where Theodahad by fair means or (mostly) foul had annexed most of the land as his private estate. Justinian was still unaware at this point that Theodahad had been raised to the throne. While Peter was journeying along the Egnatian Way on his way to Italy, he encountered envoys from Amalasuintha who told him that she had made Theodahad king, and then when he reached the Ionian Sea, he met a second set of ambassadors from Theodahad who told him that Amalasuintha had been thrown into prison. Peter reported the news to Justinian and awaited instructions. Justinian replied with a letter of support to Amalasuintha that Peter was to deliver, and he was to make no secret of its contents. But by the time he reached Theodahad, Amalasuintha was dead and Peter could only protest her murder.

The time frame of the *Secret History*'s tale is different. It relates that Peter came with secret orders from Theodora to see to it that Amalasuintha was put to death. Theodahad was a willing accomplice, and Amalasuintha, who was confined on an island in Lake Bolsena, was strangled in the bath, thereby providing Justinian with a just cause for making war on the Goths. As a reward, Peter the Patrician was given the powerful portfolio of Master of Offices, which he still held in the last year of Justinian's reign.

Both stories cannot be true, for the *Secret History* assumes that Amalasuintha was still alive when Peter reached Theodahad in Italy, whereas the report in the *Wars of Justinian* claims that she was already dead. Most historians have doubted the motive Procopius assigns the empress, and with it, her guilt. Edward Gibbon was an exception; in his *Decline and Fall of the Roman Empire* he accepted the charge, though with a quizzical footnote.

There is a scrap of circumstantial evidence among Cassiodorus' letters that suggests Theodora's guilt. We have two letters, one from Theodahad to

Theodora and the other from his queen, Gudeliva, that contain ambiguous references. Theodahad reports that he has expedited some negotiation between Theodora and the pope and continues, "For in the case of that person, too, about whom a delicate hint has reached me, know that I have ordered what I trust will agree with your intention." On the same date, Gudeliva wrote a brief, cordial letter which concludes, "an affair has arisen of a kind which should make me still dearer to your justice."[12] Theodora, presumably, understood the reference, but we do not. Was it the murder of Amalasuintha? And did Theodahad and his wife expect Theodora's approval for their foul deed?

There is another explanation. This exchange of letters took place at a time when Monophysitism came within a hair's breadth of victory. Severus, the Monophysite patriarch of Antioch who had fled to Alexandria to escape Justin I's persecution, was coaxed to Constantinople, and once there, he won the new patriarch of Constantinople, Anthimus, over to his doctrine. In Rome, Pope John II had not been inflexible. But John II was dead when these two letters were written in May 535, and Theodora anxiously awaited reports of his successor. Was he an unbending Chalcedonian? Or would he be reasonable? Theodahad was well placed to coerce the new pope Agapetus, for he had been elected with his support, and Theodora may have intimated that she would be grateful if Theodahad pressured Agapetus to be malleable. As it turned out, Theodora's worst fears were justified. Agapetus carried on the papal tradition of intractable Chalcedonianism.

Yet suspicion remains. Theodora would probably not have welcomed Amalasuintha's presence at the imperial court, where she would be a trump card in the reconquest of Italy that Justinian was planning. She might have feared that her enemies, chief among them John the Cappadocian, would find Amalasuintha a useful pawn. But if we apply the question Cicero recommended in a murder investigation, *Cui bono?* (Who gets advantage from the deed?), then high on the list is Justinian himself. Amalasuintha belonged to the Arian heresy and Justinian might have found an Arian princess an embarrassment at court at a time when he was stripping Arian churches of their wealth.[13] Moreover, he *did want* a just cause to invade Italy and destroy the Ostrogothic kingdom. Amalasuintha's murder provided one. If Theodora was implicated in Amalasuintha's death, she served Justinian's purpose.

At least the story in the *Secret History* reveals what court circles thought possible. They assumed that Theodora would feel threatened by a woman who had had the advantages of education and breeding that she lacked. Contemporaries sensed a feeling of inferiority in her makeup. Moreover, no one doubted that she was capable of plotting murder, and it is quite possible that Peter had a private conversation with Theodora before he set out for Italy and got instructions to intimate to Theodahad that Amalasuintha's elimination would not be unwelcome news at court. But before Peter reached Theodahad with his message, Amalasuintha was dead.

The Theological Dilemma

THE SEARCH FOR COMMON GROUND

The Background

With Justin's accession, the "symbol" of Chalcedon became imperial orthodoxy. "We, then, following the Holy Fathers . . . confess the one and the same Son, our Lord Jesus Christ, the same perfect in Godhead and also perfect in manhood[,] . . . consubstantial with the Father according to his Godhead and consubstantial with us according to his Manhood." The doctrine of Christ in two natures was affirmed, and Christendom was sliced into two sections: the Chalcedonians, or "Diphysites," as they were called by Severus, the patriarch of Antioch who saw barely a sliver of difference between them and the heretical Nestorians; and the anti-Chalcedonians, for whom the label "Monophysite" would eventually be coined.[1]

Eleven days after Justin's coronation, a synod of forty-three or forty-four bishops met in the capital and decided that the church councils of Nicaea, Constantinople, Ephesus, *and Chalcedon* should be inscribed in the diptychs and pronounced anathema against Severus, who had to flee for his life from Antioch. Acceptance of these four ecumenical councils of the church became the gauge of orthodoxy. For the Monophysites, the last of them, Chalcedon, was anathema.

Pope Hormisdas' delegates arrived in Constantinople early the following year, bringing Rome's terms for ending the Acacian schism and reuniting the church. But they came with instructions not to debate but to present the doctrine of Rome and demand acquiescence. On 28 March, Maundy Thursday, 519, John, patriarch of Constantinople, assented unhappily. The pope had demanded not only that the *Henotikon* be repudiated but also that retro-active anathema be meted out to the author of the *Henotikon,* Acacius, and the four patriarchs of Constantinople who were his immediate successors, as well as the emperors Zeno and Anastasius. Even the clergy who had re-mained in communion with these patriarchs did not escape condemnation.[2] The shadowy empress Euphemia emerged briefly into historical record at this point, long enough to express her opinion, which was forthright and resolutely Chalcedonian. If the four church councils were not proclaimed in the liturgical diptychs during the Eucharist, she said, she would not go to church.[3]

Hormisdas lost no time taking advantage of the new conciliatory mood in Constantinople. He urged Justin to hunt down the Monophysites and make them conform. In Antioch, the patriarch who took the place of Severus was Paul "the Jew," a tough Chalcedonian approved by the pope, and he set out to eradicate anti-Chalcedonianism in the churches and monasteries. The per-secution did not extend to the laity. Yet rooting out the anti-Chalcedonian clergy and holy men was to prove a more difficult task than either Justin or Justinian imagined. Justin himself, who was an old soldier rather than a subtle theologian, was used to dealing with subordinates who obeyed orders, and he must have been quite unprepared for the resistance he encountered when he waded into theological controversy. In retrospect, it is apparent that the early years of his reign created a breach between Monophysite and Chal-cedonian that could not be mended. The *Henotikon* that Justin discarded would never be replaced by anything equally satisfactory.

Justinian, however, was a more sophisticated theologian than his uncle, and it was not long before he began to comprehend the strength of the re-sistance. He started a search for some middle ground. It was a quest that would occupy his reign, and until her death in 548, Theodora served his pur-pose by playing a double role. On the one hand, she was her husband's ally, and pursued the same quest as he, but with the conviction that if a middle ground were to be found, the Chalcedonians must yield a little. On the other hand, her chosen role as protector of the defenseless was elastic enough to include concern for persecuted Monophysites. Her policy was ambivalent. She was both Justinian's loyal opposition and his loyal collaborator, but as long as she was alive, the Monophysites felt they had a friend at court.

In the theological milieu of Constantinople—though not in Rome—

Monophysitism was not a heresy like the others. The distinction between Chalcedonian orthodoxy and the Monophysites was expressed in small linguistic variations that signified minor differences in theological dogma, and it was a natural reaction to search for a formula to settle it all. What was needed, it seemed, was a concatenation of words that would offend no major group and avoid nouns such as "Chalcedon" and the "*Tome* of Leo,"[4] which popular rhetoric had demonized! The first was a red flag to the Monophysites, and the second was the touchstone of correct belief for the Chalcedonians. Both camps referred to themselves as the "Orthodox." Yet the struggle was linguistic only on the surface. Christianity in Late Antiquity had brought changes to society that challenged the old elites in the empire. Groups that were hitherto submerged in the all-pervasive Greek culture recovered their languages or acquired a new vulgate: in Egypt Coptic, created from demotic Egyptian with a generous infusion of Greek vocabulary, became the language of choice for the Egyptian Monophysites, and in the eastern provinces, Syriac, developed from Aramaic, played a similar role. In Antioch the success of Severus as a Monophysite evangelist was due in large part to the popularity of his Syriac hymns. He wrote in Greek, or so it seems, but it was the Syriac translations that were on Monophysite lips and have survived. Behind the Monophysite thrust there often lay a desire for self-identification and self-esteem.

To call these feelings nationalism would be an anachronism. No heretical sect in Late Antiquity wanted to establish its own nation. The Monophysites eventually started their own church with its own hierarchy, but their leaders did it reluctantly, and Theodora, whose support was critical, was anything but a percipient founder. What the Monophysites wanted was to define the orthodoxy of the whole empire, not of a sectarian movement.

In Italy and the West, however, as the secular state collapsed the pope appropriated the imperial tones of the old Roman Empire. The papacy was beyond the physical control of the emperors in Constantinople until Belisarius occupied Rome in 536, and it developed the habit of independence as well as an unrelenting determination to defend its primacy. It made the Council of Chalcedon the measure of orthodoxy, though at the same time it refused to recognize the twenty-eighth canon of the council, which gave the Constantinople patriarchate equal privileges with Rome and a rank second only to it. Rome's theology owed more to the legacy of Roman law than

Greek philosophy, and the fact that fewer and fewer theologians were fluent in both Latin and Greek meant that Rome and Constantinople looked at each other across a linguistic divide.

It was also true that in the East, there were still no barbarian settlements within imperial territory, whereas in the West, the Catholics lived cheek by jowl with them in provinces occupied by barbarian kingdoms. The barbarians were Arians, all except for the Franks, who had the least claim to civilized life. In the Vandal kingdom, the Catholics suffered persecution, which served to harden their intolerance of heresy. The Ostrogoths treated the Catholics in Italy more kindly, but they occupied the country by right of conquest, supporting themselves by appropriating the revenues from one-third of the land, and to the Italian Catholic, the papacy represented both cultural survival and self-identification. He might also feel loyal to the emperor, all the more so after Justin made his peace with the pope and the emperor was no longer a heretic. Yet the emperors were far away in Constantinople, and it was the Roman church that provided the everyday affirmation of the superior tradition of the Roman Empire and its ancient roots. Local loyalty had as much popular appeal in Italy as it did in Egypt.

Once Justin abandoned the *Henotikon*, which the emperor Zeno had promoted and Rome rejected, the search was on for a creed that would allow the Monophysites and the Chalcedonians to share the Eucharist. In 519 four well-meaning monks journeyed from the province of Scythia Minor (the Dobrudja in modern Romania) to Constantinople with a formula for theological peace. They suggested adding a codicil to the creed that would state that "one of the Holy Trinity suffered in the flesh." These words were a modified statement of the "Theopaschite" doctrine, which the Scythian monks had repackaged with enough ambiguity to make it acceptable to a Chalcedonian. Still, it had a distinct odor of Monophysitism.

It was Peter the Fuller, the Monophysite patriarch of Antioch in Zeno's reign, who had first introduced the Theopaschite proposition that in Christ's crucifixion, "God had suffered and been crucified," and introduced this formula into the *Trisagion*, which preceded the reading of the Epistle in the liturgy of the mass.[5] In Alexandria the see of Saint Mark had accepted the phrase, and in 512 the emperor Anastasius had tried to nudge the masses in Constantinople a short step toward the Monophysite camp by allowing it into the liturgy of Hagia Sophia. The result was a riot that nearly toppled him from the throne. In their monastery on the Asian side of the Bosporus, the tireless guardians of Chalcedonianism, the Akoimetoi, or "Sleepless Monks," who earned their name because they maintained an unceasing doxology by taking shifts, caught a distinct whiff of heresy. They stirred up the mob with devastating effect. The urban prefect fled for his life, and Anastasius quelled the insurrection only by showing himself without his crown in the Hippodrome, holding the Holy Scriptures in his hands.[6] The mob took pity on him, and he survived.

The same Sleepless Monks scented heresy in this new proposal too, for a formula that "one of the Trinity had suffered in the flesh" left a degree of choice: it could mean that it was God or his Holy Spirit who had suffered on the cross, having assumed flesh, as the Monophysites believed, rather than Christ in his human nature.[7] The Scythian monks were dabbling in ambiguity and using it to build a frail bridge between the Chalcedonians and the Monophysites. Yet they got a hearing before the patriarch John and the papal legates. It helped that one of them was Vitalian's relative, and Vitalian's orthodoxy was irreproachable. He had led a Chalcedonian revolt against Anastasius, and his influence at this time was paramount. Yet the papal legates were not persuaded.

But Justinian recognized possibilities in the Theopaschite formula and lent his support. From Constantinople, the monks went to Rome and stayed there for fourteen months, promoting their doctrine and awaiting the pope's approval. Hormisdas demurred, even though Justinian wrote impatiently several times urging him to make a decision. Finally the pope sent the monks packing. Justinian, however, did not forget their formula or their creative ambiguity.

Vitalian's influence was removed by his assassination in July 520. In the same year, Constantinople got a new patriarch, and the following year, the brutal Diphysite whom the pope had approved as Severus' replacement in Antioch was eased out of office. He had, it was said, murdered his archdeacon who was a Monophysite, and the murdered prelate's son escaped and got word to Theodora, who saw to it that it reached Justinian.[8] His successor, Euphrasius, was a gentler Chalcedonian and perhaps a less convinced one, though when he died horribly in the earthquake that leveled Antioch in 526, the Monophysites considered his fate deserved. Yet Justin, warned by the pope that a man who put his hand to the plow and then looked back was unfit for God's Kingdom, was determined to enforce theological uniformity, at least outside Egypt, and in 521 the persecution was renewed in earnest.

The Monophysites already knew Theodora as a friend at court, and as her influence grew, they looked to her for help. Mare, metropolitan of Amida, one of the fifty-five Monophysite bishops expelled from their sees in 521 who were relegated to Petra, sent his deacon to Constantinople with instructions to seek out Theodora and ask her for help. The year was no later than 523, and Theodora already held the rank of patrician, though she was not yet Justinian's wife. She approached Justinian, who was a Master of the Soldiers in the Presence, and he in turn approached Justin, who allowed the exiles to find refuge in Alexandria. When Mare eventually died in Egypt, Theodora saw to it that his two sisters, both deaconesses, were permitted to bring back his remains to Amida, and with them came the considerable library Mare had collected in Alexandria.[9] Yet the persecution of the Monophysites at Amida continued. Theodora as yet could offer only limited help.

Seeking a Solution: The First Phase

Once Theodora was empress, she became a more effective Monophysite ally. The persecution abated in 531, and she can take some of the credit for the policy change. She and Justinian still worked as a team, and Justinian recognized the advantage of having a wife whom the Monophysites considered accessible. Justinian and Theodora had lived in the Palace of Hormisdas at the southwest corner of the Great Palace while Justin was still emperor, and now Justinian connected the two, making the Palace of Hormisdas part of the imperial palace complex and turning it over to Theodora. She made it into a Monophysite refuge. It became a shelter for fugitive monks and clergy who migrated to Constantinople, and the palace church of Saints Sergius and Bacchus may have been their place of worship.[10] Stylite saints who had descended from their pillars, hermits expelled from their cells, and monks driven from their convents gathered there from Armenia, Syria, Isauria, Alexandria, and Byzantium itself. No less than five hundred of them migrated to Constantinople in the 530s.

They taxed the available space in the palace. The public rooms were partitioned into cells where holy men might mortify the flesh and sing hymns of praise. Theodora provided for their needs, and every two or three days she visited them and received their blessings. Justinian himself came with her on occasion, for he hoped to win their approval, and some of the holy men made a deep impression on him. On her deathbed, Theodora got a promise from him that he would care for this community of Monophysite saints, and he continued to extend them imperial protection after her death.

Justinian had begun his reign as a tough enforcer of religious uniformity. Hardly had old Justin died and left him sole emperor than he promulgated a sweeping measure against the heterodox.[11] Yet a decade of persecution had not quelled the Monophysites; on the contrary, sometime before 527 the Monophysite bishops, with Severus' assent, had decided to allow one of their number, John of Tella, to go as a missionary and ordain Monophysite priests who could administer the sacraments to believers. It was a measure that they took with hesitation. Thus far the church had had a single ecclesiastical hierarchy and only one set of clergy, and however great the divergence between Monophysite and Chalcedonian might be on matters of dogma, all the priesthood belonged to the same canonical structure. The first chink resulted from old Justin's persecution. As a result of it, there was now a Chalcedonian patriarch of Antioch and a Monophysite patriarch in exile, each recognized by his own followers. Ordaining a Monophysite priesthood was the next logical move.

But the Monophysite bishops moved slowly and reluctantly. They hesitated to make ordinations in part because they were afraid but in part too because they realized that this was a momentous step. Yet if they did not take it, the laity would be left at the mercies of a purely Chalcedonian clergy, and the Monophysite congregations could either conform or make the hard decision to refuse the sacraments. For devout Christians, the menace of eternal damnation attended such a deed.

John, a native of Callinicum on the Persian frontier, had been inspired as a youth by reading the romance of Saint Thekla, which told how a beautiful woman rejected her family and her suitors and became a follower of the apostle Paul. The bishop of Tella, fifty-five miles east of Edessa, died just as Justin's persecution of the Monophysites began, and John was conscripted as his successor. He enjoyed about two years of peace before the persecution reached his region, but eventually a rescript arrived ordering that all bishops who did not proclaim the Creed of Chalcedon in their churches should be expelled. Some bishops obeyed; many others refused and were replaced by Chalcedonians. John retired to the desert, but he did not stay there meekly. Instead, once he had Severus' permission, he began to ordain priests.

His success was spectacular. Great numbers rushed to meet him, and in sympathetic monasteries and hiding places he received candidates for holy orders. He examined them for their knowledge of Scripture and tested them for basic literacy, and once he was satisfied that they were suitable for the priesthood, he consecrated them. John crisscrossed the whole East, from Cappadocia to the Persian frontier and Persia itself, intent on his mission.

Justinian recognized the danger. A separate Monophysite hierarchy would mean a separate Christian sect and the unity of the church would be shattered. John eventually would be caught after he had carried his mission to Persia, and he died in prison in 538.[12] But he gave Justinian a glimpse of what would happen if the rift between Chalcedonian and Monophysite remained unmended.[13] Since his own method had not succeeded, he was willing to try Theodora's. In 530 or 531, the Monophysite persecution was suddenly relaxed, and Justinian and Theodora together launched a policy of dialogue.

Contemporaries were to wonder if the disagreement of Justinian and Theodora on theology was genuine, or if it was politically inspired. Possibly it was both. Theodora's Monophysitism was the result of a sincere conversion, whereas Justinian's Chalcedonian beliefs were the result of a Catholic upbringing in a province of the empire that acknowledged the supremacy of the pope. At this point they worked hand in hand; it was not until the 540s that Theodora acted more independently, or at least appears to do so. The persecution that Justin initiated had driven Monophysite holy men out of their monasteries and stylite saints off their pillars, and not all retired to the desert. Some had been accepted as martyrs in the villages, which were growing both in size and in importance for the resurgent native cultures that did not use Greek. The Palace of Hormisdas offered the Monophysite leaders refuge and at the same time kept them under control, for it curbed their freedom of movement. Yet the Palace of Hormisdas was also a space where there might be a dialogue under imperial supervision between Monophysite churchmen and their Chalcedonian counterparts.

The exiled Monophysite bishops, John of Tella among them, were recalled from the desert and summoned to Constantinople. On their arrival, they presented an address to the emperor. It was their duty, they said, to obey when commanded, and hence they had left their desert refuge and come peaceably to the feet of the emperor and his "God-loving queen," on whom they prayed God to bestow good gifts. They had no wish to be disputatious; rather they wanted to present a reasonable confession of their faith that Christ incarnate had one nature and it was divine. Not two natures, one divine and the other human. "Just as an ordinary man," they asserted, "who is made up of various natures, soul and body and so forth, is *not* divided into two natures, because a soul has been joined by composition with a body to make up the one nature and person of a man, so also God the Word, who was personally united and joined by composition with soul-possessing flesh, is not divided into or in two natures because of his union and composition with a body." They could not accept the Council of Chalcedon, they explained, for it contradicted the verdict of the earlier Council of Ephesus that had condemned Nestorius, who confessed Christ in two natures, and it violated the first ecumenical council at Nicaea that had been convened by Constantine the Great himself.[14]

In the Chalcedonian camp, Theodora was a recognized enemy. She was regarded with suspicion and hostility. The biography of Mar Saba, the archimandrite of the Great Lavra of Mar Saba near Jerusalem and a doughty Chalcedonian, records an incident that illustrates the Chalcedonian consternation. The saint, now more than ninety years old, came to Constantinople in 531 and was greeted respectfully by Theodora, who asked for his blessing and his prayers that she might become pregnant and have a child by Justinian. Mar Saba's retort was brutal.[15] He would not pray that she conceive and give birth, lest she breed another enemy of Chalcedon! To his followers he expressed the hope that no fruit would come from Theodora's womb, for he feared that her offspring would nurture the heretical doctrines of Severus and restore the policies of the emperor Anastasius, thus bringing a host of evils upon the church.

The conversations between the Monophysites and the Chalcedonians went on for more than a year, and in 533 they held a formal debate in an audience chamber of the Palace of Hormisdas, which lasted three days. Justinian himself attended on the final day. Six bishops represented the Chalcedonians, led by Hypatius of Ephesus and Demetrius of Philippi, and in their group was a cleric we shall meet again, the bishop of Trapezus (Trebizond), Anthimus, a theologian much respected for his asceticism, who preferred to live in Constantinople rather than his own see. On the Monophysite side, John of Tella was the principal cleric, and Justinian and Theodora tried hard to win him over.[16] The first day looked into the origin of the dispute and it went well enough. Monophysite theology went back to Eutyches, the abbot of a monastery in the suburbs of Constantinople who had denied that Christ had two natures even after he became a man and walked on earth. The debate in the Palace of Hormisdas reached a consensus that Eutyches was too extreme. His condemnation by the Council of Chalcedon had been correct.

But on the second day, rifts appeared. The central doctrine of Chalcedon was the double nature of Christ. He was both man and God while he was on earth. The Chalcedonians were a little embarrassed by the bald wording of their creed, for the heretic Nestorius had preached a doctrine that had emphasized the human nature of Christ to the extent that its followers denied the Virgin the title "Theotokos" (Mother of God), for it implied that she had given birth to a deity. At the first Council of Ephesus in 431, Nestorius was condemned, deposed as patriarch of Constantinople and exiled. The Chalcedonians tried to distance their Diphysitism from the extreme Diphysitism of the Nestorians. Yet it was not easy to draw a boundary between the two. It was made no easier by the hard fact that the Council of Chalcedon had restored two of Nestorius' strong supporters to their bishoprics: Theodoret of Cyrrhus and Ibas of Edessa.

Yet the Chalcedonians managed a reasonable defense. They pointed out that the council had insisted that before Theodoret and Ibas were returned to their sees, they had to condemn Nestorius. The Monophysites pressed the matter no further. But they had made a valid point and the Chalcedonian rebuttal left something to be desired.

On the third day, Justinian himself was in attendance, and he attempted to breathe some life into the Theopaschite formula as a basis for reconciliation. Pope Hormisdas had rejected it, but the Scythian monks had probably continued to promote it, though we know nothing of their activities after Hormisdas dismissed them from Rome. But Justinian did not gain much for all his efforts. One bishop defected from the Monophysite camp, as well as some priests and monks, but for the most part, both camps stood firm. The gulf between the two remained unbridged. The eastern clergy went home, including John of Tella, who continued his evangelism in Persia until he was captured and imprisoned.

Yet Justinian still had hopes for the Theopaschite solution. The next year he addressed an edict with a distinct Theopaschite flavor to thirteen cities, none of them in Egypt where he did not expect opposition. Without rejecting the Council of Chalcedon, the edict managed to skirt around the central tenet of Chalcedonianism: the dual nature of Christ incarnate. It condemned both Nestorius and Eutyches, who were demonized as the authors of extreme Diphysitism and extreme Monophysitism respectively. A delegation was dispatched to Rome to present this statement of faith to the newly elected pope, John II, and John proved flexible.

John's retreat on the Theopaschite question had overtones of policy. Pope Hormisdas had been free to take a hard line. It had paid off in the short run; he had ended the Acacian schism on his own terms. The epitaph on his tomb, composed by his son Silverius, celebrated his victory: "Greece, vanquished by godly authority, has yielded to you."[17] But Pope John's power base was less secure. His immediate predecessor, Boniface II, had left a divided church. Boniface's election was suspect: he had been ordained in one basilica in Rome while a rival was ordained in another. The rival died within a month, and Boniface pronounced anathema against him. The clergy who had supported the rival—the majority—reacted bitterly. Then Boniface attempted to choose his own successor, an ambitious deacon named Vigilius whom we shall meet again. But Boniface was forced to backtrack. When he died, two and a half months of negotiation elapsed before John was chosen, and his election was tainted by suspicions of simony.[18] The papal see was in need of healing. Justinian's delegation of Greek clergy headed by two bishops, Hypatius of Ephesus and Demetrius of Philippi, was a welcome distraction, all the more so because they brought rich gifts.

Even so, John did not give approval right away. The Sleepless Monks had also sent a delegation and John made a vain attempt to try to win them over to Justinian's profession of faith. In November 533 the impatient emperor reissued the edict he had addressed earlier to only thirteen cities, this time sending it to the main metropolitan sees, including Rome and Thessaloniki where Rome claimed jurisdiction. But John chose to overlook the emperor's lack of restraint and did not take offense. On 25 March 534, he gave his approval, and Justinian's statement of faith was duly made law and incorporated into the second edition of the *Codex Justinianus*, which was promulgated in November of the same year.[19] As for the Sleepless Monks and their adamantine Chalcedonianism, the pope at last lost patience and excommunicated them.

Then Justinian summoned Severus. He had refused Justinian's first invitation, saying he was old and infirm,[20] but now he yielded. He was reluctant to leave Alexandria, for he thought nothing could be achieved, but Justinian's letters were urgent and Theodora was persuasive. He braved a midwinter voyage from Egypt to come. Theodora welcomed him and his party and lodged them in the palace. They had much to discuss, and it was not merely theology, though Theodora was an eager student. On 7 February 535, the patriarch of Alexandria, Timothy III, had died, just after Severus set out for Constantinople. Theodora had regarded Timothy as her spiritual father, and she was determined that he have a worthy successor and, it goes without saying, a Monophysite.[21]

The Monophysites who gathered in Constantinople took full advantage of Theodora's protection. Justinian and Theodora may have hoped to keep them isolated, but they made their presence felt in the city. John of Ephesus [22] reports that they attracted great crowds, and some Chalcedonians actually renounced their creed. He may have exaggerated, but theology was a burning issue, and the Palace of Hormisdas housed some very charismatic holy men.

From his monastery near Amida, the stylite saint Z'ura, who had been forced to come down from his pillar by the persecution, set out for Constantinople and arrived in 535 with ten disciples. He was a man of proven sanctity; it was reported that once a marauding Hun had raised his sword to kill him and found his arm frozen in place until the saint consented to release it. Chalcedonian informers had already sent word to Justinian to beware; this was a holy man who was both charismatic and combative. Even so, Justinian was unprepared for his boldness. Z'ura accused him of spilling the blood of the faithful and warned him of the Day of Judgment so bluntly that Justinian lost his temper.[23] But he did not dare arrest him. Instead he fulminated that the Council of Chalcedon had made a true decision, and if the teachings of Z'ura and his disciples were not false, then let God show a sign to prove it. In an outburst of fury, he threatened death for those who denied Chalcedon.

Then Z'ura replied heatedly that Chalcedon was anathema not only to his followers but to the angels in Heaven as well. Believers needed no sign to prove it; still, for Justinian, Z'ura promised a portent that Justinian himself would recognize. Justinian left the audience hall in a rage. But the next day, the story goes, he developed a great wen on his head that grew until he no longer looked or acted like a human being. Theodora took charge immediately. She secreted Justinian in an inner chamber with only two physicians and two chamberlains in attendance, and let no one else see him. Then she sent a message to Z'ura to beg intercession. Z'ura came, recognized the wen as a sign from God, and prayed for Justinian. In the same hour, Justinian's delirium left him, and out of dread for Z'ura, he granted his demands. But, adds John of Ephesus who relates this story, the state of the church he did not set right.

Yet Theodora was very pleased with Z'ura. She chose him to administer the rite of baptism to her,[24] and she gave him a large villa in Sycae (modern Galata), north of the Golden Horn. Z'ura transformed it into a monastery and settled there with his disciples, under Theodora's protection.

Events moved swiftly. The year 535 witnessed the deaths of three patriarchs of the church. In February Timothy III of Alexandria died. Four months later it was the turn of Pope John II, and a month later came the sudden death of Epiphanius, patriarch of Constantinople. It had been he who had crowned Justinian and Theodora, and he was a loyal Chalcedonian without being stiff-necked about it. His death was unexpected, but it opened an opportunity, and Theodora seized it. A successor was quickly found, and he was Theodora's man. He was the bishop of Trapezus, Anthimus, who had been a member of the Chalcedonian team in the debate two years earlier in the Palace of Hormisdas. He roused no anxiety in the Chalcedonian camp, for his loyalty to the Chalcedonian Creed had never been doubted, though probably Theodora was aware that he gave only lukewarm support to the doctrine of two natures. He was her candidate, and she smoothed the way for him. There was a church canon that forbade the translation of bishops from one see to another, but it was no impediment, though the Chalcedonian monasteries in Constantinople and Jerusalem noticed Anthimus' transgression and sent protests to Rome.

Theodora was also the go-between who brought Anthimus and Severus together, and the two men discussed the theological impasse. Anthimus was easily persuaded. Severus was the abler theologian, and in any case Anthimus was sympathetic. He gave Severus a letter with a Monophysite confession of faith and sent another to the newly elected patriarch of Alexandria, Theodosius. The patriarch of Jerusalem went along. Theodora's conniving seemed on the point of bearing fruit.

Severus too wanted peace, even though he had come to Constantinople expecting to achieve nothing, and his discovery that Anthimus was a secret sympathizer must have been an agreeable surprise. Severus was now the recognized leader of mainstream Monophysitism that was more or less satisfied with the *Henotikon*, which the emperor Zeno had promoted and old Justin discarded.[25] In the eyes of the Monophysites, Severus was still the legitimate patriarch of Antioch. Yet within Egypt itself, his influence was modest and his following dwindling. By this time the majority of Egyptian Monophysites had switched allegiance to a new theological star, Julian, bishop of Halicarnassus, who, like Severus, had fled from his see to Alexandria to escape the persecution of the emperor Justin. But once there, he split with Severus and developed an extreme form of Monophysitism that held that Christ had not merely a single nature that was divine but that the divine nature had so absorbed the flesh that his body escaped corruption. Severus, on the other hand, never denied that Christ had two distinct natures, insisting only that they were so closely united that his will had only a single existence. Far from denying Christ's humanity, he stressed that his human frailties proved that he had a body of a human being, created at birth and subject to dissolution in the grave after death. He felt no animus against Rome, though he abominated Pope Leo and his *Tome*.

The Julianists, or Aphthartodocetists or Phantasiasts as they were variously known, attacked Severus and his followers from one side, calling them Phthartolatrae, that is, worshipers of Christ's corruptible body, while the Chalcedonians attacked him from the other. Yet the gulf that separated Severus' doctrine from the ideology of Chalcedon had become, if anything, narrower than that which yawned between it and Julianist dogma. However, for Severus and his followers, the sticking point was still the "symbol" of Chalcedon, with its bald assertion of the double nature of Christ. The Monophysites had demonized the very word "Chalcedon."

Yet Severus was not disloyal to Justinian: he too believed in one empire and one faith, but he was not prepared to have that faith defined by the Chalcedonian Creed. If the memory of Chalcedon could be expunged, there was hope for a settlement, and Severus must have welcomed the prospect of bridging the schism that divided Christendom as much as Justinian. For Theodora, the consensus Severus and Anthimus reached was a triumph for her policy.

Yet the applause was anything but universal. The Chalcedonian patriarch of Antioch, Ephraem, was appalled at this collusion between Severus and Anthimus and the defection of the patriarch of Jerusalem. Ephraem had been a soldier before he became patriarch, and he brought a soldier's mindset to the job of enforcing Chalcedonianism within his see. The monasteries in Palestine were no less alarmed. Mar Saba was dead, but his Lavra was the intellectual center of the Palestine monasteries, and it was firmly Chalcedonian. And what of Rome? Pope John II was dead, and his successor, Agapetus, was still an unknown quantity. Ephraem of Antioch sent Agapetus a message to report his fears and anxieties.[26] Theodora also sent a message to the new pope and another to the Roman senate, and she notified the new king of the Ostrogoths, Theodahad, who had just rid himself of Theodoric's daughter, Amalasuintha, and was anxious at this point to appear cooperative.[27] Theodahad replied in a letter crafted by Cassiodorus[28] that he had ordered the pope and the senate to reply without delay. John II had not been inflexible; he had accepted the Theopaschite doctrine. What of Agapetus? Theodora would soon find out.

In fact, the auguries were not good. Agapetus, who belonged to a great Roman family that had already given the church one pope, was an old man when he ascended the throne of Saint Peter, and his many years and his awareness of Rome's imperial legacy made him overbearing. It was soon clear that he would have no truck or trade with heresy. In Africa, he faced the problem of the Arian clergy. Now that Africa was recovered and the Arian regime of the Vandals destroyed, some of the Arian clergy switched to orthodoxy and expected to be integrated into the Catholic hierarchy. It was hard to forgive or overlook the persecution the Catholic priesthood had suffered at the hands of the Vandals; yet accepting the Arians would have been a statesmanlike policy. Agapetus would have none of it.

In the prefecture of Illyricum, where the patriarch of Constantinople and the papacy competed for control, Agapetus was prepared to assert Rome's rights. Justinian had renamed his natal village Justiniana Prima (modern Cariçin Grad) and raised its bishop to the rank of metropolitan without consulting Rome. Agapetus warned him sternly that that would not do. Agapetus was prepared to resist even emperors when he thought it necessary. With the Ostrogothic kings, however, the popes could not afford such a degree of independence. Justinian was about to launch an attack on the Ostrogoths, ostensibly because Theodahad had murdered Amalasuintha, and Theodahad mandated Agapetus to go to Constantinople to effect a reconciliation. Agapetus obeyed Theodahad's command, although he had to pawn some of the Holy See's treasures with Gothic brokers to pay his travel expenses.

In 536 Agapetus reached Constantinople and received a gracious reception from Justinian and Theodora. Yet within the brief period between his arrival in March and his death on 22 April, he demolished the consensus that Theodora had contrived between Severus and Anthimus. Presumably he mentioned the commission Theodahad had assigned him, but he wasted little time on it; in any case, Justinian had by now made up his mind to invade Italy. Instead Agapetus assailed the Monophysite apostasy that he found in the capital. Justinian threatened him with exile and Theodora did her utmost to win him over, but Agapetus would not budge. He would not even receive Anthimus at all unless he could prove himself orthodox, and even then, he recognized him only as the bishop of Trapezus, for he would not condone bishops moving from one see to another. He even accused Justinian himself of yielding to heresy, and in his own defense Justinian signed a *libellus* asserting that he was a true Chalcedonian Catholic. Yet Agapetus would not accept Anthimus into communion, and he would not be intimidated by any fulmination from Justinian. "Sinner that I am," he replied to him, "I have long wanted to come to the most Christian emperor Justinian—but now I have encountered Diocletian; yet I am not in the least afraid of your threats."

Justinian then confronted Agapetus with Anthimus, and Agapetus brusquely demanded that the patriarch admit that there were two distinct natures in Christ. Anthimus demurred. Thereupon Agapetus excommunicated him. He excommunicated Severus too, and probably Theodora as well.[29] Indeed, he included in his denunciation the whole congregation of Monophysites gathered in the Palace of Hormisdas.

Justinian yielded. The war against the Goths was getting under way, and he could not alienate the pope at this juncture. Moreover, unlike Theodora, he was not disloyal to Chalcedon, and he accepted Rome's prerogative to define orthodoxy. It was not unimportant that Justinian and Agapetus shared Latin as their native tongues.[30] He abandoned Anthimus once he refused to admit two natures in Christ as the pope demanded, and in his place Agapetus consecrated Menas, the director of the Hospice of Samson, which was the chief hospital in Constantinople, situated between the churches of Hagia Sophia and Hagia Eirene.[31] Unable to win over Justinian, Anthimus took off his pallium and laid it on the altar in the emperor's presence, departed, and disappeared.

Severus escaped with Theodora's help and returned to Egypt, where he retired to the desert. Two years later he died at Xois in the Delta where a supporter had give him refuge on his estate. His biographer, John of Beith-Aphthonia,[32] relates that as he suffered from his final illness, his friends tried to persuade him to take a bath to cool his fever. He refused, for, he said, ever since he had taken up the monastic life, he had never looked upon his naked body. In the end, however, he agreed to take a bath, clothed. The sarcophagus made for him was found to be too small, but while his attendants discussed what to do, they found that his body fitted after all. Either by divine intervention his cadaver had shrunk, or the stone sarcophagus had grown.

Agapetus had no time to savor his victory, for on 22 April 536, he died so suddenly that the Monophysites attributed it to God's wrath.[33] But the five Italian bishops and two Roman deacons who had accompanied Agapetus remained until their business was completed. They met with representatives of the patriarchates from the East in a council that Menas convened in the year of Agapetus' death on instructions from Justinian. Anthimus was summoned but was not to be found anywhere. Thereupon he was deposed. Justinian guessed that his wife had moved Anthimus to a safe house outside the city, but he preferred not to make a search for him. Not until Theodora died twelve years later was it discovered that she had hidden him in the women's quarters of the palace.[34]

Theodora's game plan was in ruins. But in the strongholds of Chalcedonianism there was rejoicing. The monasteries in Constantinople, the deserts of Jerusalem, the three provinces of Palestine, Second Syria, and Mount Sinai, whose abbots had assembled in the capital, addressed a letter to the new patriarch, Menas, wherein they lauded the judgment against Anthimus and Severus and added wild accusations of the assorted standard crimes that the ecclesiastical mind attributed to heretics.[35] In the East the persecution of the Monophysites was renewed with fresh vigor, spearheaded by the relentless patriarch of Antioch, Ephraem. Justinian returned to his policy of imposing Chalcedonian doctrine by force when necessary.

In Alexandria, however, the struggle was within the Monophysite camp itself. When Timothy III died, Theodora's chamberlain, Calotychius, was on the spot and saw to it that Timothy's secretary, Theodosius, was chosen to succeed him. But his investiture was interrupted by a popular uprising in favor of the archdeacon Gaianus, a Julianist. Theodosius narrowly escaped assassination and had to flee the city. When word reached Theodora, she approached her husband. The author of the *Liber Pontificalis* of the Alexandrian popes, Severus of Ashmounein,[36] remarked that Justinian was secretly glad that the Monophysites in the see of Alexandria were at each other's throats, but he yielded to Theodora and gave her leave to send her favorite,

Narses, to Alexandria. Narses, with six thousand troops at his back, dis-
lodged Gaianus after only 104 days on the patriarchal throne and restored
Theodosius.

But the mob fought back. Theodosius hung on for sixteen months, and
Narses had to fight a civil war to support him, at one time even setting fire to
part of the city to quell the Gaianist rioters. Finally, in autumn 536, Theodosius abandoned Alexandria for Constantinople. Gaianus, however, did not
win; he died in exile in Sardinia, and though the Copts remained split between Gaianists and Theodosians beyond the end of the seventh century, it
was the latter who would eventually prevail.[37]

Yet in the struggle between Theodora and Pope Agapetus for Justinian's
allegiance, Theodora had lost. The pope had yielded on one small point: he
did not repudiate the Theopaschite doctrine that his predecessor, John II,
had accepted. But he reclaimed the emperor for Chalcedon and revived his
determination to enforce it. Egypt now would no longer be exempt. When
Theodosius reached Constantinople in autumn 536, he met Justinian and
Theodora, and Justinian did his utmost to persuade him to accept the Creed
of Chalcedon. But he refused. Justinian persuaded and threatened and ca-
joled for a year before he finally lost patience. For the first time he used his
imperial authority as God's vicegerent to remove a patriarch without consulting a synod or a council of the church. Theodosius was deposed and
sent off along with some three hundred Monophysite clergy to a fortress at
Derkos in Thrace, thirty miles from Constantinople, where Theodora made
them as comfortable as she could. In Theodosius' place, Justinian appointed
a stoutly Chalcedonian monk from a Pachomian monastery in Egypt, thus
ending a span of fifty-five years during which the see had been headed by
Monophysites.[38]

Theodosius, thirty-third patriarch of the see of Saint Mark, was never
to return to Alexandria. Yet, ironically, in exile from his see he won the acceptance that was denied him while he was there. By the time of his death
in Constantinople in 567, the Monophysites recognized him as their leader
and the spiritual successor of Severus. In Alexandria itself, the Chalcedonian whom Justinian had appointed patriarch might have physical control
of the churches, but Theodosius in exile controlled the hearts and minds of
the Egyptian church.

Theodora's Quest for a New Strategy

Rome Triumphant

Theodora would have been only human if she took some satisfaction from Pope Agapetus' fate. The biographical sketch of Z'ura by John of Ephesus describes the encounter of these two resolute clerics. Agapetus complained to Justinian about the charismatic stylite saint who enjoyed Theodora's protection, and Justinian gave him a free hand to deal with him as he would. Agapetus set out in a boat across the Golden Horn to Z'ura's monastery in Sycae with a band of troops, but the wind drove them back and finally a bolt of lightning struck the boat. But in spite of this signal from Heaven, Agapetus continued to utter his blasphemies, as the Monophysites considered them, and his tongue began to swell. Twice the swollen tongue was lanced, but in vain; the pope died on 22 April.[1] But Justinian and Theodora were unnerved by the great numbers who flocked to Z'ura's monastery and confined him at Derkos along with the other Monophysite churchmen whom they removed from Constantinople until the embers of the dispute died down.

The story tells us more about Monophysite perceptions than actual fact. Yet it appears that Agapetus' tongue did mortify and he died, though not before he inflicted a sharp defeat on the Monophysites. Dante, who placed Justinian in the Second Sphere of Paradise, has him pay tribute to Agapetus, who saved him from theological error. The tribute has a documentary basis, for we have the edict that Justinian addressed to the new patriarch Menas, denouncing the heretics Severus and Anthimus, and along with them Z'ura and Peter of Apamaea, who was one of Severus' most loyal partisans.[2] It reads, in part,

Justinian to the most holy and blessed Menas, archbishop and ecumenical patriarch: In proceeding to the present law we are taking a course not unfamiliar to the imperial power. For every time that the clerical vote has promoted to the episcopal throne any persons unworthy of the sacred office, such as Nestorius . . . and Arius and others not their inferiors in wickedness, the imperial power has always come to the support of the priesthood, to the end that through our right judgments things divine and human may blend to form a single harmony. Something of this sort has, as we know, been recently done in the case of Anthimus, who was driven from the episcopal throne of this imperial city by Agapetus of sacred and renowned memory, who was at that time prelate of the most holy church in old Rome, on the ground that Anthimus, in violation of all sacred canons, had usurped the throne which in no way belonged to him, though he had been condemned and deposed alike by the decree of the aforesaid man of sacred memory, and by the holy synod held in this place, because he had departed from the true doctrine and abandoned the tenets which he appeared to accept, making many pretenses that he conformed to the four sacred councils,[3] though, in fact, he did not accept their findings nor take advantage of our kindness and condescension which we had displayed.

So much for the luckless patriarch, Anthimus, who lay concealed in the women's quarters of the same palace where Justinian issued his edict. It then proceeded to place Severus under anathema. "And we further forbid anyone," Justinian wrote,

to possess any of his writings; and just as no one is allowed to copy or possess the writings of Nestorius . . . so also let not the writings of Severus be kept in the home of any Christian, but let them be counted profane and alien from the Catholic church, and let them be burnt by their possessors unless those who have them wish to put themselves in peril. And let them not be copied hereafter by any copyist, whether he be one who makes fine or rough copies, nor anyone else whosoever; for the penalty for anyone who makes a copy of his works is the cutting off of his hand. And likewise we absolutely also forbid this man to approach the imperial city or its neighborhood or any other of our more important cities, but we command him to settle in some desert spot and not corrupt others or lead them into blasphemy or be always devising something new against the true faith, whereby he might strive once more to bring confusion on our most holy churches.

Yet Theodora had lost a battle, not the war. It was not long before she managed to have the exiled Monophysite clergy transferred from Derkos to the relative comfort of the Palace of Hormisdas, and there Theodosius was to remain until his death in 567. Theodora's support did not falter, and in the years ahead a subtle alteration appears in the old working relationship between her and her husband. She would not abandon her Monophysite clientage, and Justinian accepted that. But their visions of the future diverged. Justinian still hoped for a new *Henotikon*, that is, a softened Chalcedonianism free from any trace of the Nestorian heresy, which would win the support of moderate Monophysites. The extremists would have to be coerced. Theodora was willing to lend Justinian her support, but she was also ready to move tentatively in the direction of a separatist option, which would be a second-best solution but no longer an unthinkable one. That is, she was prepared to accept two separate divisions of Christendom, one Chalcedonian and the other Monophysite, each with its own priesthood and bishops and both joined in allegiance to an emperor who was the vicegerent of God.

The Monophysites under her protection, however, were prepared to take advantage of their patron. John of Tella was put to death by Ephraem, the patriarch of Antioch, in 538, but his biographer, John of Ephesus, concludes the sketch of his life by saying that God raised up another John to take his place.[4] The second John was the bishop of Hephaestopolis in Egypt. He was a Palestinian monk from Gaza who was driven from his monastery by the persecution and came to the great Monophysite center at Ennaton, a cluster of monasteries at the Ninth Milestone from Alexandria. He attracted Theodosius' notice during the sixteen months that he clung to the patriarchal throne of Alexandria with Narses' troops to protect him, and Theodosius ordained him a bishop. He came to Constantinople with Theodosius and went along with him into the detention center at Derkos.

Life for the Monophysite churchmen confined at Derkos was not comfortless, thanks to Theodora's patronage, but in return for her support, she expected them to refrain from ordaining priests; if they did not, she could not protect them from the death penalty. John could not endure this constraint. He asked Theodosius for leave to visit Constantinople, claiming he was ill. He got authorization, and Theodora gave him quarters in the city and a living allowance. He began to ordain priests. Reports of what he was doing reached Theodosius, who denied that he had given John any permission to make ordinations: Theodora, he said, had taken responsibility for John and he washed his hands of the whole business. Then some of John's enemies contrived, under false pretenses, to get a written order from Theodora for him to leave Constantinople and presented it to John, telling him that he must depart immediately and not try to see the empress; otherwise he would die. But John was no fool. He pretended to make preparations for his departure but instead slipped off to the palace and came into the presence of Theodora herself. The truth came out. Theodora threatened John's accusers with punishment, but John came to their defense. However, Theodora commanded John to remain in the palace and ordain no more priests.

The wily bishop agreed. But he asked permission to go to a villa outside the city for a month or so for the sake of his health, and in fact, his health was poor. But instead of remaining at the villa, he slipped away to Asia and got as far as Tarsus, never spending more than a day in one place, all the while contacting Monophysite believers and making ordinations. From Tarsus he intended to go into Syria, but the authorities learned that there was an unidentified renegade bishop ordaining priests, and the stern patriarch of Antioch, Ephraem, and his bishops sent a complaint to Justinian. Suspicion fell on John, but Theodora herself gave evidence that he had been sick in a villa outside Constantinople. So while Ephraem was given orders to arrest the unknown bishop, he was also assured that no bishop from the Palace of Hormisdas had left the city. So John traveled to and fro from Constantinople as far as Palestine and Alexandria under the protection of Theodora, who did not know, or pretended not to know, that he had even left the capital.

Justinian, however, now decided to impose a patriarch on the see of Saint Mark in Alexandria, and his choice fell on a monk named Paul from Tabennisi in Upper Egypt, where there was a monastery founded by the father of cenobitic monasticism, Pachomius. The Pachomian monasteries were nurseries of Chalcedonianism. There was little hope of having a peaceful consecration in Alexandria itself, and so the Chalcedonian whom Justinian appointed to the see was consecrated in Constantinople by Menas, and thus, unintentionally, he began a tradition whereby the Chalcedonian patriarchs of the see of Saint Mark would receive their consecration in Constantinople.

Paul moved energetically. The author[5] of the chronicle of the Coptic patriarchs reports the Monophysite version of events: the people of Alexandria would not receive Paul, and Justinian retorted by sealing the doors of the churches. The people went without the sacraments for a year and then began, secretly, to build Monophysite churches for themselves. Thereupon Justinian reopened the churches and put them under Chalcedonian control. The truth seems to be that in less than two years, Paul reduced Monophysite worship in Alexandria to only a couple of churches, and in the countryside his harsh tactics won over many of the monasteries. The conversions may not have been sincere, but the church in Egypt submitted for the moment.

Paul had been the suggestion of the papal legate (*apokrisarius*) in Constantinople, Pelagius, for after Agapetus' visitation, the papacy had reestablished its permanent legation at the imperial court. The patriarchs of Alexandria, Antioch, and Jerusalem all had legates, but Rome had withdrawn its nuncio at the time of the Acacian schism, and once the schism ended in 519, the office was not immediately restored, perhaps because relations between Constantinople and Theodoric became chillier as the king grew older. Pelagius was a smooth apparatchik who rapidly gained influence at court. He got Justinian's ear, and he learned how to keep in Theodora's good graces, even though he was not a theological ally.

His skill served him well in 540 when Paul of Tabennisi was accused of the murder of an obdurate deacon and brought to Gaza for trial before the patriarchs of Antioch and Jerusalem. Pelagius, acting as Rome's representative, was among the judges. The case was a complicated one in which Theodora played a devious role. Paul, tired of his deacon's obstruction, had handed him over to the Augustal prefect, a man of Phoenician origin named Rhodon, who had orders from Justinian to support Paul in every way. The luckless deacon was tortured, and whether it was intended or not, he died on the rack. Theodora was horrified and insisted that Paul be brought to trial.

He was not proved guilty, but nonetheless he was deposed and replaced by a monk from Palestine named Zoilus, who lasted until a popular insurrection drove him out in late 546. Zoilus was a simple man, and less harsh than Paul the Tabennisiote, but he was a Chalcedonian. Pelagius saw to that, while still managing to avoid offense to Theodora. The unfortunate prefect Rhodon, who *did* offend Theodora by carrying out his orders too zealously, became the sacrificial lamb: he fled to Constantinople where Justinian beheaded him and confiscated his property.[6] Another associate of Paul of Tabennisi was crucified; he was a Samaritan named Arsenius who had converted to Christianity after the Samaritans revolted in 529 and his sympathy for them had been too overt. However, he took his new religion too seriously; he studied Christian theology and became a vigorous Chalcedonian. Theodora, who had favored him once, turned against him and ordered him impaled.[7]

Theodora's Riposte

In Italy Theodora saw a chance to salvage the entente that Pope Agapetus had destroyed. She was never in any doubt that if there was to be theological peace, Rome would have to be more flexible, and she failed entirely to comprehend the unswerving loyalty of the Catholic West for the Chalcedonian Creed. A new pope had to be elected, and in Agapetus' entourage there was the upwardly mobile deacon, Vigilius, the same man whom Pope Boniface had once tried unsuccessfully to choose as his successor. Vigilius belonged to a Roman senatorial family with ambition bred in its bones; his father had been a praetorian prefect and his brother an urban prefect, both in the service of the Ostrogothic monarchy. He still coveted the papal throne, and he sought Theodora's help. He evidently promised her in writing that if he were chosen, he would reverse the excommunication of Anthimus. But before Vigilius could return to Rome, King Theodahad had his own favorite candidate elected. Silverius was the son of the stiff-necked Pope Hormisdas (514–23), whose term had overlapped the last years of the emperor Anastasius and the early years of Justin's reign. Silverius knew how to win the support of Theodahad, whose fondness for money was his salient characteristic. He gave him a bribe to win his support, and Theodahad secured the assent of the Roman clergy by threatening to kill them if they failed to choose Silverius.

Theodora was foiled only for the moment. The conquest of Italy was already under way in 536. Naples, abandoned by Theodahad, fell to the Byzantine invaders under Belisarius, and the Ostrogoths, disgusted by their king's incompetence, dethroned him and chose instead an experienced soldier named Witigis. He had to face a double threat: Belisarius was advancing from the south, but in the north, Justinian had incited the Franks to invade Italy. Weighing the odds, Witigis decided that Belisarius' little army was the lesser menace. He left an adequate garrison in Rome, and having extracted loyalty oaths from the pope, the senate, and the people, he departed for Ravenna where he married Amalasuintha's daughter and made peace with the Franks.

Once Witigis was gone, Silverius switched allegiance adroitly and urged the Romans to open their gates to Belisarius. On 9 December 536, a Byzantine army occupied Rome. Justinian and his general Belisarius were in Silverius' debt. Thanks to him, the small army that Belisarius led did not have to lay siege to Rome, which would have been a difficult operation in the winter months. But Silverius had incurred Theodora's dislike. What mattered to her was that Silverius was the son of the pope who had pursued the Monophysites relentlessly in the early years of old Justin's reign and, equally important, that he stood in the way of her plans.

According to the potted biography of Silverius in the *Liber Pontificalis*, Justinian sent the new pope a letter inviting him to Constantinople where he might void the excommunication of Anthimus, and Silverius sent his reply, not to Justinian but to Theodora: "Lady empress, to restore a heretic who has been condemned in his wickedness is something I can never bring myself to do." Theodora then plotted his downfall. Her instrument was Antonina, the wife of Belisarius, and Antonina acted with the same vigor and lack of scruple that she was to show a few years later when she brought down the praetorian prefect John the Cappadocian. Rome was under siege. Witigis had never intended Rome to fall into Byzantine hands and he marched on the city with 150,000 men and kept it under siege for a year and nine days. Belisarius had only 5,000 troops. Silverius was a valuable ally whose allegiance was beyond doubt, for he had broken his oath of loyalty to King Witigis and could not have been eager to meet him again. He was an unlikely traitor. But Antonina followed Theodora's instructions, which were to depose Silverius, whatever the consequence for the military campaign.

Rumors were floated about that the pope was corresponding secretly with Witigis. Finally Belisarius summoned Silverius to the Pincian Palace where he was staying and he and Antonina interviewed Silverius alone in an inner room. Antonina took charge. Why, she demanded, did Silverius want to betray them to the Goths? Thereupon, without any chance to protest his innocence, he was taken to a side room, and as Vigilius looked on, he was stripped of his *pallium* and dressed as a monk. A subdeacon came out to the clergy waiting outside and told them that the pope was deposed. Vigilius took over. The next day, 25 March 537, he was elected, consecrated, and enthroned as pope. Belisarius saw to it that the operation went smoothly.

Silverius was dealt with pitilessly. He was banished first to the city of Patara in Lycia, in modern Turkey, but the local bishop was indignant at the maltreatment Silverius had undergone and reported his case to Justinian, who, it appears, knew nothing about the plot Theodora had carried out. He did not approve, and he sent Silverius back to Rome with orders that Belisarius review the accusations against him and, if he was innocent, restore him to his pontifical seat. The smooth papal nuncio Pelagius won Theodora's favor by opposing the move: let Silverius stay in Patara, he advised, perhaps guessing what his fate might be in Italy.[8] Once Silverius reached Rome, Belisarius turned the matter over to his successor, Vigilius, who imprisoned him on a little island in the Tyrrhenian Sea and fed him on the "bread of affliction and the water of distress," as the *Liber Pontificalis* puts it. He died of starvation on 2 December 537.

"Then," reports the *Liber Pontificalis,* "the empress Theodora wrote to pope Vigilius, 'Come now, keep the promise you made us of your own free will about our father Anthimus, and restore him to his office.'" But Vigilius proved no more flexible than Silverius, even though the redoubtable Antonina pressed him hard.[9] He did not deny his promise, but now that he was the vicar of Saint Peter, he claimed that he could not revoke the anathema that Popes Agapetus and Silverius had upheld. Anthimus, concealed in the women's quarters in the imperial palace, would wait in vain for rehabilitation.

Even granted that our knowledge of Vigilius reaches us through a veil of hostile sources, he cuts a poor figure. His ambition had led him into an alliance with Theodora, and he made promises he could not keep in return for her support. Now he had become pope, he realized that the Italian clergy would sooner desert him than the uncompromising Diphysitism of the Chalcedonian Creed. Moreover, now that Africa was restored to the empire and its Catholic bishops to their churches, they reinforced the Diphysite position. There had always been a certain rigor to the African church, and the persecution that the Catholic clergy had endured under the Vandals had not enhanced whatever tolerance they had. They were unyielding partisans of Chalcedonian dogma. Caught between a resolute empress in Constantinople and an inflexible clergy on his home turf, Vigilius adopted what seemed to be the wiser choice, which was to satisfy the clergy at home and keep his contacts with the imperial court to a minimum.

Meanwhile, the war against the Ostrogoths in Italy dragged on. In 538 Narses arrived in Italy with an army of five thousand troops to help Belisarius. His star had been rising since Theodora sent him to Alexandria to protect Theodosius against the Gaianists, and his failure to control the Gaianist mob had not damaged his career. Justinian held him in high regard, and Theodora considered him a person she could trust.[10]

Narses and Belisarius soon fell out. It is impossible to discern Theodora's fine hand here, for the quarrel brought her no advantage. Rather it was a spat between two prima donnas, and it injured the war effort. Narses' reluctance to cooperate with Belisarius was the chief reason for the fall of Milan to the Goths in March 539 and the horrific massacre that resulted, wherein one of the victims was Pope Vigilius' brother.[11] As a consequence, Justinian recalled Narses. He returned to Constantinople to the politics of the imperial court, where he was a dexterous player, and in 541 he performed a bit part in the scenario that brought down John the Cappadocian.

Belisarius took Ravenna in 540, though he did it by tricking the Goths into thinking he would rebel and make himself king of Italy if they surrendered the city to him. Justinian and Theodora looked on with displeasure. Justinian would probably have preferred a negotiated peace in Italy that would preserve a truncated Gothic kingdom in the Po Valley where it could serve as a buffer between Byzantine Italy and invaders from the north. But Belisarius wanted a triumph and was determined to take Ravenna. Justinian, however, was in no mood to grant Belisarius a triumph. When he returned to Constantinople with his imperial airs, and the Ostrogothic treasure, he got a cool reception.

Justinian and Theodora had other important business to absorb their attention in the year that Ravenna fell. A horde of Kutrigurs and Slavs had surged across the Danube. One force pushed south as far as the Isthmus of Corinth; the other took Cassandreia, threatened Thessaloniki, and pushed on as far as the walls of Constantinople itself, spreading panic in the city.[12] In the East, the Persian king Khusru chose the same year to invade. Antioch was sacked, and before the city fell, the Chalcedonian patriarch Ephraem made a swift exit from it that was both adroit and ignominious. Monophysite tradition had it that Antioch's fate was divine retribution for Ephraem's blasphemy: he had gathered 132 bishops from his see in Antioch for the dedication of a new church and made them all confirm in writing their acceptance of Chalcedon and anathematize Severus.[13] The destruction of Antioch followed in due course.

For Theodora, the immediate problem was John the Cappadocian. She was locked with him in a struggle for power, and even her urgent warnings to Justinian had not brought him down. In 540 his career was at its height. One would like to believe that Theodora's chief motive for plotting his fall was a high-minded desire for good government, as John the Lydian suggests in the brief mention Theodora gets in the surviving part of his *On the Magistracies*.[14] Perhaps that was a subsidiary motive. But her overriding objective was to remove a threat to her power. Once John was removed, she could act more independently.

The Founding of the Jacobite Church

In Italy the first phase of the war against the Ostrogoths had ended in 540, with the fall of Ravenna. Yet the Goths were not beaten, and they soon realized that Belisarius had tricked them into giving up their capital. They determined to find a new king and fight on, and after two false starts, they found a king called Baduila (as he names himself on his coins) or Totila, as Procopius calls him. He was a far abler man than the luckless Witigis whom Belisarius had defeated, and it was not long before the Byzantines were beaten back and the Goths were again in control of most of Italy. Justinian's plan to restore the empire in the West turned sour. But it was in the East that the immediate crisis loomed. Antioch had suffered earlier destructions before its sack in 540, but they had been acts of God. Earthquakes and fires were frightening and costly, but they did not damage imperial prestige. The Persian sack did. Justinian's regime had failed utterly to defend the premier city of the East. Its Chalcedonian patriarch, Ephraem, had fled. Bishops of other cities in the path of the Persian invasion had tried to protect their flocks, particularly the brave bishop of Aleppo, ancient Beroea, but Ephraem was not one of them. The detached prose of the historian Procopius quivers with indignant bewilderment as he described the destruction of Antioch by Khusru and the enslavement of its citizens: "I cannot comprehend why the fortune of a man or a place is, by the will of God, lifted up on high, and then overthrown and destroyed for no reason that we can see. For it is not right to say that everything is not always done according to divine reason, and yet it allowed a man who was utterly unholy to raze Antioch to the ground."[15]

The following year, the Ghassanid emir, al Harith ibn Jabalah, was in Constantinople on other business and took the opportunity to seek Theodora's help.[16] He wanted a Monophysite bishop for his tribe. John of Tella and his successor, John of Hephaestopolis, had ordained Monophysite priests, but thus far no Monophysite bishops had been consecrated. Once that step was taken, a separate Monophysite hierarchy could become a reality, for bishops could consecrate more bishops and a synod of bishops could choose patriarchs. Harith was asking Theodora to take a giant step.

Yet we have no evidence that she hesitated. Nor can we be sure that she consulted Justinian, and perhaps she did not, though Justinian might not have opposed her if she did. Harith's goodwill was important, for the Ghassanids guarded the southern Syrian frontier and allowed Justinian to concentrate imperial forces in the northern sector. At this point, the empire's need was desperate. When Harith asked for an orthodox bishop, by which he meant a Monophysite one, there was no snubbing his request. Theodora smoothed the way. Theodosius, who lived under her protection in the Palace of Hormisdas, consecrated two bishops, Jacob Bar'adai as metropolitan of Edessa and Theodore as metropolitan of Bostra. Both were nomadic bishops, and though they were notionally attached to cities, they did not live in them. Theodore followed the rovings of the nomadic Ghassanids as they moved between their southern and their northern pastures. Bar'adai had a greater destiny.

Jacob Bar'adai (ca. 500–78), who emerged from a cell in Constantinople where he had lived for fifteen years, became one of the great missionaries of all time and would give his name to the Jacobite church.[17] He was born in Tella, the son of a priest named Theophilus bar Manû, and he became a monk and a disciple of Severus at an early age. Shortly after Theodora became empress, he came to Constantinople with a fellow monk named Sarkis (= Sergius) to beg her to help the persecuted Monophysites, and there he stayed for fifteen years. Now he accepted ordination as bishop of Edessa, the metropolis of the province of Osrhoene, though he did not dare go into the city itself. Theodora could not have saved him from arrest if he were caught by the imperial police, and Ephraem, the Chalcedonian patriarch of Antioch, would try hard to capture him but without success. Instead John flitted from place to place, ranging on foot from the Persian frontier all the way to Constantinople, organizing clergy and ordaining priests, continuing the mission that John of Tella had begun. He was a master of disguise; his name

Bar'adai came from the coarse horse cloth, in Syriac, *bárá'thân*, which was his usual costume. He passed for a beggar and his disciples never betrayed him.

Within a few years he ordained thousands of priests and deacons; tradition mentions eighty thousand. More important for the future of the church: he also consecrated thirty bishops, and in 557 he made his old friend Sarkis, the Monophysite patriarch of Antioch, the successor of Severus. He extended his mission to Egypt, where he ordained twelve new bishops, and held a secret synod in Alexandria to organize an Egyptian Monophysite church.

The church he organized was not Greek but Coptic, and the Jacobite church in Syria and Mesopotamia used the Syriac language. These churches thrived on protest culture: they represented the ethnic groups whose ancient civilizations had been submerged by the Greeks, and they defined their distinctness by minor differences in dogma and ritual. For instance, they made the sign of the cross with only one finger, thus signifying that Christ had a single nature. They coexisted with the parallel Chalcedonian ecclesiastical structure, the "Melkite" church. That is, the church that belonged to the emperor, for the label is derived from the Syriac word for "king." The Monophysite churches did not. Nor did they belong to Jacob Bar'adai; by 559 two of the bishops whom Jacob had consecrated at his secret synod in Alexandria were on a collision course with him on matters of doctrine and founded a new Monophysite sect, the "Tritheists," one of whose "True Believers" was Theodora's grandson, Athanasius.

It was in 541 that the Ghassanid emir Harith approached Theodora with his request for a bishop, the same year that Theodora engineered the fall of her hated rival, John the Cappadocian. But it was in 542 or 543 that Bar'adai began his mission. So it may well have been the plague that struck the East in 541 and the capital in 542 that steeled Theodora to take the momentous step she did. Justinian took ill, and for a brief period, Theodora had to face the danger that her husband would die and her power base disappear. She gathered imperial authority into her own hands, and during this period of crisis, it must have been she who took charge. Her sharp reaction when news reached her that the army officers in Oriens were discussing Justinian's successor while Justinian lay ill shows how insecure she was.[18] All her authority would evaporate if Justinian were to die. Who then would speak for the Monophysites? It may have been an overwhelming sense of doom that led

Theodora to act as independently as she did and become cofounder of the Jacobite church, for without her intervention Jacob could not have begun his mission.

But Justinian survived the plague year and outlived Theodora by seventeen years. The pandemic dealt heavy losses to the population, and the empire that carried on was poorer and overextended. We, from the vantage point of the twenty-first century, interpret plagues and wars in terms of demography and economics and tend to overlook the mass psychology of the time, which is more difficult to grasp. But in the empire of the mid-sixth century, the Devil walked abroad. When the plague reached Constantinople, people saw demons on the streets.[19] The *Secret History* reported a story that a monk—perhaps a Monophysite—came to the imperial court to seek relief for his neighbors who were suffering wrongs, and as he was being ushered into the audience hall, he froze with horror on the threshold, for he saw the Prince of the Devils himself sitting on the throne![20]

Yet, even now that Heaven had expressed its dissatisfaction by inflicting pestilence upon God's people, the regime trudged on, all the more determined to find a solution to the theological divisions that split the empire. Theodora spent the rest of her life loyally seconding Justinian's effort to wring some concessions from the pope so as to bridge the gap between the Chalcedonians and the Monophysites. It was not a wide gap, but it was guarded jealously by the mass psychology of the contending parties. As for the church that Theodora launched, it solidified the rift, which was a result that she probably did not intend. By the time Justinian died, the Jacobite church had set up a clandestine hierarchy in opposition to the Melkite church and chose its own patriarchs from among its loyal monks, thus continuing the succession through Severus, whose deposition the Monophysites never recognized, back to Saint Peter himself, the founder of the Antioch church. The Jacobites learned to endure oppression, and the experience stood them in good stead when Islam took over the East in the next century.[21]

The Coercion of Rome

After Pope Agapetus' death in 536, the new patriarch of Constantinople, Menas, convened a synod that formally deposed Anthimus. Two churchmen who attended were the Palestinian monks Theodore Askidas and Domitian, leaders of the Origenist faction in Palestinian monasteries. Mar Saba had warned Justinian about the Origenists in Palestine when he visited Constantinople in 531, but now the saint was dead, and the Origenist numbers were increasing. The sixth-century Origenist revival was the work of a monk from Edessa, Stephen bar Sudaili, who died in about 543. Origen himself belonged to the third century. He was a prolific author and perhaps the most brilliant of the early Christian thinkers; he had been appointed director of the theological school of the see of Alexandria, the so-called Didaskaleion, before he was twenty. Excommunicated in 231-32, he took refuge in Caesarea Maritima in Palestine where he continued his teaching. When persecution broke out in midcentury under the emperor Decius, he was arrested, tortured, and finally put to death, probably in the year 254. Origen and the founder of Neoplatonism, Plotinus, came from the same intellectual matrix, and the new Origenism of Stephen bar Sudaili was a tribute to the Neoplatonic legacy of mysticism that had already worked its way into Christian thought.

Stephen bar Sudaili met such opposition in Edessa that he moved to Palestine where he made converts. In his old age, Mar Saba had grown worried at the growth of the movement. But Justinian was an eclectic theologian, and Theodore Askidas and Domitian captured his attention when they attended the synod of 536. He made the former bishop of Caesarea in Cappadocia and the latter bishop of Ancyra, modern Ankara.[1]

The struggle between the Origenists and the anti-Origenists in the Palestinian monasteries broke into the open in 539, and the next year six of the most obdurate anti-Origenists were expelled from the Great Lavra and took refuge with Ephraem, the patriarch of Antioch. The struggle moved to the imperial court. The shrewd papal nuncio, Pelagius, had already taken the measure of Justinian and understood the power of a little flattery when it concerned the emperor's theological competence. In 543 Justinian promulgated an imperial constitution addressed to Menas, patriarch of Constantinople, in which he set forth ten anathemas against Origen.[2] It was a most satisfactory exercise, both for Justinian and for Pelagius who inspired it. The constitution, which is more a manifesto than a law, displayed Justinian's theological competence, and all the patriarchs signed without demur. Theodora paid no great attention; while Justinian was composing his constitution with Pelagius' help, she was laying the foundation of the Jacobite church.

Theodore Askidas and Domitian survived easily enough. Both put their signatures on Justinian's decree, gritting their teeth as they did so, perhaps, but it was that or lose their influence at court. Pelagius could claim the outcome of the affair as a personal victory. He departed for Rome with the considerable fortune he had acquired in Constantinople and left the field free for Theodore Askidas to repair his damaged prestige and plot his revenge.

Meanwhile, in Rome, Pope Vigilius concerned himself with papal duties within his own see and maintained politic silence as far as the emperor was concerned. The less communication with Constantinople, the better. It was not until September 540 that he sent Justinian and Menas the profession of faith that popes customarily sent upon their elevation. He had the confidence of Belisarius, who appointed the pope's brother Reparatus praetorian prefect of Italy in 538. The following year, when Milan fell to the Goths, the unfortunate prefect was captured and killed and his flesh fed to the dogs. But Theodore Askidas, with Theodora's support, plotted a new theological departure that would trap Vigilius between the emperor and the unyielding Chalcedonianism of Rome.

The "Three Chapters" dispute began with a suggestion of Theodore Askidas to the emperor. One accusation that the Monophysites flung against the Chalcedonians was that they were tainted with the heresy of Nestorianism, and what Theodore suggested would refute the charge. There was some substance to it. When the Chalcedonian Creed was decreed at the Council of Chalcedon in 451, Nestorius, by then an old man in exile at the oasis of

El Khargeh in Egypt, found it so near his own doctrine that he could think of no objection.

Nestorius had been a product of an Antiochene school of theology that, a century before Severus took over the see, had preached a doctrine that laid special emphasis on the dual nature of Christ. The founding theologians were Ibas of Edessa, Diodorus of Tarsus, and Theodore of Mopsuestia. Diodorus was the earliest of the three. He was a native of Antioch who had gone to school in Athens before he became a monk, and he moved from being the abbot of a monastery to the bishopric of Tarsus in 378. He stressed both the perfect divinity and the perfect humanity of Christ. The human Christ was merely the shrine wherein the Divine Logos dwelt, and thus the Virgin Mary gave birth only to the man Jesus Christ, not to God. The proper epithet for her, according to Diodorus, was *anthropotokos:* "she who gives birth to a man." The epithet, "Theotokos," that is, Mother of God, would not do.

Theodore, bishop of Mopsuestia (ca. 350–ca. 428), was a disciple of Diodorus and was in turn the teacher of Nestorius. Theodore Askidas had a private reason for wreaking vengeance on his memory, for he had been an enemy of Origenism, and achieving his posthumous anathematization would even the score with Pelagius.[3] Finding that Justinian was already hard at work on a treatise with which he hoped to entice some of the Monophysites into the fold, Askidas planted the notion in his head that the best way to achieve what he wanted was to free Chalcedonianism from any hint of the Nestorian heresy. That could be done by condemning the bishop of Mopsuestia and along with him, two others of his school, Theodoret of Cyrrhus (ca. 393–ca. 466), who had defended Nestorius and been deposed and exiled for it but had later been restored by the Council of Chalcedon after he anathematized Nestorius, and Ibas of Edessa, who had translated Diodorus and Theodore of Mopsuestia into Syriac. Theodoret and Ibas had both opposed Cyril, patriarch of Alexandria, the greatest theologian of the fifth century and Nestorius' opponent. What Justinian was persuaded to aim for was to make Cyril's teachings central to a new *Henotikon,* which both the Chalcedonians and the Monophysites could accept.

And Theodora's motives? No doubt she hoped that her husband would be successful in his quest, for she was loyal. Besides, Severus and his disciples had treated Cyril's teachings as almost canonical, and a new *Henotikon* based on them must have seemed attractive. But Theodora cannot have been very sanguine. Yet she lent Askidas her support, for what he wanted to do was to correct an error that was made in the Council of Chalcedon, and she realized better than Justinian that if the hated council could be shown to be in error on one point, then it might be vulnerable on others. What is more, all political considerations aside, any verdict reached within the pure realm of unadulterated theology must have agreed that the writings of Nestorius' defenders were heretical. The Chalcedonian defense in the "Three Chapters" dispute was built on weak grounds.

But the empress also had private reasons. In her view, Roman intransigence was the sticking point that prevented a new *Henotikon*. Vigilius, in whose interests she had dethroned Pope Silverius, had proved to be an ungrateful, obdurate prelate, and the opportunity to bend him to her will was welcome. With her encouragement, in 544 Justinian published a treatise in the form of a long edict under three headings, or "chapters," to use the word in a specialized ecclesiastical sense. It condemned Theodore and all his works, Theodoret and his polemics against Cyril, and Ibas for a letter in Syriac that he wrote to the Mari, the bishop of Ctesiphon in Persia. A Greek translation is extant, of all his works the only survivor.

The patriarchs were unhappy. Stephen, the papal nuncio who was Pelagius' successor, urged Menas of Constantinople to refuse to put his signature to the edict, and Menas did hold out briefly; even when he yielded at last to imperial pressure, he made the reservation that he would retract if the pope refused to sign. Ephraem of Antioch and Zoilus of Alexandria followed his example. Peter of Jerusalem came to Constantinople, bringing with him a memorial in defense of Theodore of Mopsuestia that the anti-Origenist monks of Palestine had produced. It infuriated Justinian, and the unfortunate Peter had to turn for help to Theodore Askidas, who saw to it not only that the patriarch signed the edict but also that the Origenists in the Great Lavra got the upper hand again. Pelagius' previous victory was reversed. In this game of theological snakes and ladders, Askidas mounted a ladder while Pelagius slid down the slimy back of a snake. More was to come.

The Resistance of Vigilius

Pope Vigilius balked. He had limited choice. The Latin bishops, including Vigilius himself, did not know Greek and could not read the writings that were being condemned. When it came to the fine points of theology, they were at sea. But they recognized the "Three Chapters" edict as an attack on the Council of Chalcedon and solidly opposed it. Rome's supremacy was at stake.

Justinian determined to bring Vigilius to Constantinople. The war was not going well in Italy, and it was important that Vigilius should not be shut up in Rome, cut off by the Goths, while the dogmas of the church were being negotiated. On 25 November 545, as Vigilius was celebrating mass in the church of Santa Cecilia in the Trastevere region of Rome, he was arrested. He went willingly enough. He was put on a riverboat, and as his craft floated down the Tiber to the sea, the Romans lined the riverbank and jeered. Vigilius, they realized, was escaping the rigors of a renewed siege.

He interrupted his voyage in Sicily and remained in Catania for about ten months. He did not forget the Romans he had left behind: he sent them a convoy of grain harvested from the papal estates in Sicily, but it was captured by the Goths who killed all the crew members and passengers except the bishop Valentinus to whom Vigilius had entrusted the spiritual government of the city. His hands were amputated, but his life was spared.

Vigilius used these months in Sicily to take soundings, and what he discovered steeled his resolve to resist Justinian. The hostility of the Latin bishops to the condemnation of the "Three Chapters," particularly those in Africa, was sharp. Illyricum did not like it at all. A message arrived from the patriarch of Antioch saying that he had signed only under compulsion, and a legation reached Catania from Zoilus of Alexandria who asked pardon for having assented to the decree. When Vigilius reached Constantinople on 25 January 547, his reception was splendid. The pontiff and the emperor embraced and kissed each other, weeping with joy, and as they made their way to Hagia Sophia, the crowd cheered. But soon Vigilius was engaged in a contest of will with both the emperor and the empress.

Theodora had not much longer to live, but she threw her remaining energy into the quarrel. The papal nuncio in Constantinople had already excommunicated Menas, and Vigilius confirmed the excommunication. He also excommunicated the bishops who had supported Justinian's edict, and perhaps he excommunicated Theodora as well. Theodora did not yield. Argument did not melt Vigilius; so Theodora and Justinian turned to coercion. Vigilius bent a little. He settled his quarrel with Menas. And he wrote a secret letter to Justinian and Theodora saying that he personally condemned the "Three Chapters" but feared that an anathema would harm the rights of Rome. The following year, in April, he issued a *Iudicatum* that condemned the "Three

Chapters" and at the same time upheld the Creed of Chalcedon, thus trying to straddle the issues. On 28 June, Theodora died.

The opposition to the "Three Chapters" edict no doubt saw Theodora's death as a just punishment from God, and they became bolder. Vigilius faced a rebellion of practically all the Catholic bishops of the Latin rite. In Africa the bishops met in a general council and broke off communion with the pope. The pope retorted with anathemas, but it did no good. In Illyricum the metropolitan of Justiniana Prima, Justinian's birthplace, was deposed by his bishops for supporting the condemnation of the "Three Chapters." The emperor made a prudent retreat. The war was not going well in Italy, and he could not afford to alienate the Latin church. He allowed Vigilius to repudiate his *Iudicatum*, but in return he got a secret agreement from him that he would work for the condemnation of the "Three Chapters."

But Vigilius still resisted, and in 551 Justinian issued a second edict against the "Three Chapters." Intense negotiations followed. At one point, Justinian tried to have the pope arrested as he said mass in the church of Saints Peter and Paul, but the pope wrapped his arms around the ambo and while Justinian's posse tugged, he held on tightly until the ambo toppled over and his frustrated abductors departed quickly, for the onlookers in the church were becoming hostile. Just before Christmas, Vigilius fled across the Bosporus to Chalcedon, where he took refuge in the church of Saint Euphemia. The patron saint of old Justin I's empress, the stoutly Chalcedonian Euphemia, took Vigilius under her protection.

But eventually Justinian had his way. The Fifth Ecumenical Council opened in Hagia Sophia in May 553. Vigilius was not there, but his resistance was weakening. He issued a decree condemning the writings *allegedly* written by Theodore of Mopsuestia and Theodoret of Cyrrhus. But Justinian recognized this as a surrender that left the pope a loophole and would not accept it. The council condemned Vigilius, and in February 554 Vigilius capitulated and gave his unqualified consent. He had fought a good fight, and when he set out for home, he was a broken man suffering from kidney stones. He died on the way, in Syracuse.[4] But the Latin church was not prepared to forgive him. When his body reached Rome, it was denied burial in Saint Peter's, where the other sixth-century popes were interred. The rift between the Chalcedonians and the Monophysites remained as wide as ever.

Theodora did not live to witness the pope's defeat. The African chronicler Victor of Tonnena, who was in Constantinople at the time, reported that she died of cancer. He used the Latin word *cancer* (crab), which Roman doctors used to describe spreading growths that caused excruciating pain. Modern medicine might diagnose differently,[5] but we may be not far wrong to suspect breast cancer as the cause of Theodora's death. Yet however great her agony on her deathbed, she did not forget her refugee Monophysite churchmen whom she protected in the Palace of Hormisdas. They would become vulnerable once she was dead, and indeed the Chalcedonians barely waited for her to be laid to rest before they attempted to oust them from their quarters. But Theodora got Justinian to swear that he would look after them, and he kept his oath.

Afterword

Theodora's Achievement

The war against the Ostrogoths was going badly in spring 548, as Theodora lay dying, though the news of her final illness had not yet reached Italy. The Goths had found an exceptional leader in Totila, who had snatched the initiative from the Byzantines. Belisarius needed additional troops desperately, and in the aftermath of the plague, soldiers were scarce. Justinian had sent two thousand foot soldiers, but it was not enough, and Antonina left Italy for Constantinople to beg Theodora to intervene and find the necessary reinforcements. But when she arrived, she found Theodora already dead. Thereupon she realized that she had no further hope of achieving anything and urged Justinian to recall her husband. Justinian complied readily, for, claimed Procopius, he gave priority to the war with Persia.[1]

The story is instructive for two reasons. First, it casts doubt on the conventional wisdom of historians who assert that Justinian was dazzled by his conquests in the West and wasted resources on them, whereas Theodora believed that the sinews of the empire were in the East and had little confidence in her husband's policy of *reconquista*. In fact, Justinian was starving the Italian front in the 540s, whereas it was Theodora who was open to argument on the need to commit more resources to Italy, or so Belisarius and Antonina thought.

Second, the story illustrates the mode of governance at the imperial court. Even a general with a great reputation who desperately needed reinforcements had to find an advocate with authority and influence who was willing to listen, if he was to get additional help. In 548 Theodora was the only hope that Belisarius' Italian campaign had. The "Three Chapters" dispute was in high gear in Constantinople and absorbed Justinian's attention. Pope

Vigilius had given qualified consent to the condemnation of the "Three Chapters" in his *Iudicatum* of April 548, which he withdrew after Theodora's death, but at the same time he, along with the other Italian notables who had sought refuge in Constantinople, kept pressing the emperor as hard as they could to send more troops to Italy and end the long agony of the Gothic War.[2] Yet Antonina's considered opinion was that there was only one lobbyist at court with enough clout to persuade Justinian to take notice, and that was his wife, Theodora. Once her intervention was ruled out by death, the wiser course for Belisarius was to abandon a theater where failure was inevitable.

Yet the aftermath is not what we might expect. After Justinian recalled Belisarius at the request of Antonina, who judged the Italian war a lost cause, he made a new attempt to deal with the Italian problem without Belisarius. It was almost as if Theodora's death and Belisarius' recall had cleared the decks for a fresh approach. Justinian put Theodora's old enemy Germanus in command of the war against the Goths. Germanus died before he could reach Italy, but as part of his preparations, he married Matasuintha, the last descendant of Theodoric the Ostrogoth, and sired a child. It appears that he was about to try a new strategy that would reach out to the Ostrogoths and take them into partnership. Theodora's death had freed Justinian to authorize his cousin to attempt a solution that hitherto had been blocked by her enmity for Germanus and the threat she perceived that Germanus' family posed for her own.

Yet when Germanus died and his fresh approach perished along with him, Justinian turned to Theodora's old protégé, Narses, who was a back-room veteran of the imperial bureaucracy. He demanded and got the resources that Belisarius was denied. Italy was ruined, but Narses finally brought the war to an end in 552. It was an ephemeral triumph, for three years after Justinian's death, the Lombards invaded Italy. But it proved that without Theodora at his side, Justinian could still act effectively. Perhaps even more effectively.

Justinian's pursuit of theological peace was an arena where he must have missed Theodora, in spite of their variant opinions. As Justinian grew older, theology became an obsession. Theodora had been an anchor who could return him to the day-to-day problems of the empire, and once she was dead, his obsessive behavior increased. They had shared an ability to find able men to carry out their policies, but the ability faded once Justinian was old and alone. His officers and civil servants grew old along with him. The African poet Corippus, writing just after Justinian's death in praise of his successor,

Justin II, noted that before Justinian died, he had ceased to care about things of this world.[3]

With the evidence we have, it is hard to separate Theodora's policies from Justinian's, and little wonder. Contemporaries were equally perplexed by the meaning of their partnership. In ecclesiastical affairs, Justinian seems to have been convinced that what separated the Chalcedonians and the Monophysites was a purely theological question, and it could be solved by treatises, edicts, and synods, provided only that the right formulas could be found. He was fascinated by the subtle argumentation of theology. Theodora was no ignoramus in theological matters, but her comprehension of the subtleties was less sure.[4] However, she did grasp very clearly the popular perceptions of the quarrel and the passions that propelled it.

She understood the contention between the Monophysites and the Chalcedonians in terms of party rivalry, where the partisans, like fans at a football game, defined themselves as supporters of one team or the other. It was a deadly competition, for it was embittered by religious enthusiasm, and the prize offered was eternal salvation. Nonetheless, it was the ecclesiastical equivalent of the contests between the Blue and Green teams in the Hippodrome. Theodora's party was the Monophysites and Justinian's the Chalcedonians, and the contest was not played on a completely level field, for Justinian, for all he coerced Vigilius and became the archetypal caesaropapist of modern history books, still respected the papacy. He wanted the pope on his side, not because he was coerced, but because he had been convinced by argument. Theodora did not share his respect; in her view, Vigilius was simply a slippery, compromised team captain.

If that was Theodora's assessment, she was not entirely wrong. Religious enthusiasm in Late Antiquity reached all levels of society and was an outlet for emotions that had little to do with theology. If the Latin bishops had been able to read the writings of Theodore, Theodoret, and Ibas and had studied them with open minds, they might have agreed that Justinian had a point when he argued that they were heretical. But what the Latins saw in the "Three Chapters" dispute was an attack on the Chalcedonian Creed and the primacy of Rome. In the East, where Monophysitism had its most numerous adherents, the quarrel widened the rift between the two sects, for there the heresy fed on resentment against Rome and a papacy that had inherited the imperial manner of the Roman emperors. If the dispute had taken place in the nineteenth or twentieth century instead of the sixth, we would recognize nationalism as the driving force behind it, but in the age of Justinian, nationalism was an anachronism. Nonetheless, the Jacobite church in Syria and Mesopotamia and the Coptic church in Egypt was to owe much to irredentist enthusiasms.

Probably Theodora knew this better than Justinian. The difference between them went back to their early beginnings. Justinian was born in a Latin-speaking enclave in the Balkans and as a boy learned to respect the authority of the pope and accept Rome's right to define orthodoxy. An anathema from the pope was something to be feared. Not so Theodora. She spent her youth in the theater, which monks and priests abominated and where they were sometimes ridiculed in return, and she was converted in Alexandria where Rome's interdicts had little effect. She knew that if the split between the Monophysites and the Chalcedonians was to be mended, it could not be altogether on Rome's terms, and she saw nothing wrong with compelling a pope to bend a little.

She did her best, and Latin tradition hated her for it. There is a notion among historians that Monophysitism was a dying force until Jacob Bar'adai was unleashed by Theodora upon the eastern provinces. "Through his [Bar'adai's] untiring activity he breathed life into what seemed a mere expiring faction," writes one authority,[5] and it is true that in the course of the sixth century the Monophysite communities *within* the Byzantine patriarchate were crushed one after another, and what survived were the separate churches of Egypt and the eastern provinces. Would Monophysitism have died out completely without Theodora's intervention, which made these separate churches attainable? It is not impossible. If so, the history of the next century might have followed a different course, for the Monophysite split inadvertently helped to pave the way for the spread of Islam.

The historian of the Catholic Counter-Reformation, Cardinal Baronius, recognized Theodora as a particularly deadly foe of Catholic Christendom and attacked her in a masterpiece of vituperative prose.

> Such as these were the evil schemes that were the work of this degenerate woman [Theodora], another Eve who heeded the serpent, and who was the source of every ill her husband endured. She was another Delilah working with cunning and deceit to enfeeble the strength of Samson, another Herodias thirsting for the blood of holy men, and a replica of the saucy maidservant of the High Priest who tempted

Peter to deny his Lord. But it is not enough to revile her with names of that sort, for she surpassed all human women in impiety. Rather let her take from the devils in Hell a designation such as that which mythology gives to the Furies. We should choose the name of the mad woman Allecto, or Megaera or Tisiphone. She was a denizen of the Abyss and mistress of Demons. It was she who, driven by a satanic spirit and roused by diabolic rage, spitefully overthrew a consensus that was won with great toil, and a peace redeemed by the blood of martyrs and seconded by the sweat of confessors.

The vituperative cardinal wrote before Procopius' *Secret History* was discovered in the Vatican Library and revealed Theodora's early life as a demimondaine. The *Secret History* would have delighted Baronius, for Procopius' judgment of Theodora was as devastating as his own. Here was a historian who prefigured Baronius himself! The violent hatreds that Theodora provoked in the Counter-Reformation merely reflected the passions she aroused in her own day.

But if the Catholic church reviled her, among the Monophysite churches in the East there was a different verdict. There she was revered. John, the Monophysite bishop of Ephesus, called her "the Christ-loving Theodora, whom God perhaps appointed queen to be a support for the persecuted against the cruelty of the times."[6] For him, she was the "believing queen" who visited the Palace of Hormisdas every two or three days to receive the blessing of the Monophysite churchmen lodged there.[7] Michael the Syrian,[8] Jacobite patriarch of Antioch in the twelfth century, saw her as the faithful empress who worked for the peace of the church. But the churches she helped to found were overtaken by Islam, and the ruined monasteries and crumbling churches in the old prefecture of the Orient that can still impress the traveler, are evidence of a religion in steep decline.

Theodora played the game of politics skillfully, pressing her advantages as far as she could but never compromising her loyalty to Justinian. Even the acerbic Cardinal Baronius paid her a backhanded compliment. How happy Justinian would have been, he wrote, if he had had a good Catholic woman with Theodora's abilities as his consort instead of the heretic that he married.[9] Yet her achievement should never be overestimated. Justinian listened carefully to her counsel and even paid tribute to it.[10] But Justinian and Theodora were not equally matched rulers, for in the last analysis, the reins of power were in his hands, not hers. She could not be a Queen Elizabeth I or a Catherine the Great.

What is more, her influence was never paramount except in the year of the plague. Justinian had other advisers. As long as John the Cappadocian was praetorian prefect, Theodora possessed a rival who had Justinian's ear almost as much as she did. When John fell into the trap Theodora set for him with Antonina's help, it was even rumored that Justinian gave him a chance to save himself. Certainly he was reluctant to abandon him, for he valued his prefect's ability. He let John go because he had compromised himself, not because of Theodora's dislike. The scheme that Theodora and Antonina devised showed that John's ambition outweighed his loyalty to his imperial master. He had ceased to be trustworthy.

As for Theodora, Justinian had no doubts. The reason that he accepted her as a partner in power and let her act with such independence that at times the two seemed to go in opposite directions was that he never doubted her complete loyalty. Even if we were to discount romantic love as the glue that held them together, which we should not, self-interest bound Theodora to Justinian. Without him, she was only an aging onetime comedienne from the theater.

She remains a fascinating figure. "Hers is at once a striking rags-to-riches story, a tale of palace intrigue and ruthless machinations, and yet also a record of her own genuine convictions and nuanced participation in the work of government."[11] She was born into the dregs of society. Her education was sketchy. Yet she attended imperial councils and debated questions with Justinian before the senate, though Procopius suggests sourly that the debates were staged.[12] She quickly learned how to construct a power base for herself and used it to challenge the old senatorial elite that disdained her origins, and she created her own network of supporters, clients, and informers, using for the purpose, one suspects, both Monophysite churchmen and old friends from the theater. Her knowledge of theology was less profound than her husband's, but she could hold her own in discussions. She brought her family into the imperial elite and found good marriage partners for them, and she did not forget her old friends of the theater. The laws that stigmatized them in the past were changed for the better.

Justinian promulgated a number of measures to amend the double standard for men and women of the Roman legal system. A woman had had the right to conduct her own business without a male guardian since the reign of

Constantine; with Justinian, the right was extended: a widow could now be the guardian of her own children. Women's property rights were recognized. The rules were made the same for dowries and antenuptial donations. There is a concern for public morality in Justinian's legislation on marriage and the family that probably owes something to Theodora. Divorce by mutual consent could no longer be tolerated; instead Justinian listed the legitimate grounds for separation of man and wife. A husband had the right to kill his wife's lover but only after he had sent him three written warnings, duly witnessed.[13] Adultery remained a crime, but for the first time in the history of Roman law, Justinian used detention as a punishment. A wife caught in adultery might no longer be slain but would be shut up in a convent, and she could leave only if her husband pardoned her within two years.[14] There is both a dislike of the death penalty and a streak of puritanism in Justinian's family law. We cannot guess the exact degree of Theodora's input, but we can be certain that as long as she was alive these laws were a product of her discussions and debates with her husband.[15]

In 559, eleven years after Theodora's death, Constantinople itself came uncomfortably close to being captured by an incursion of Kutrigurs led by their khan, Zabergan, who led tham across the frozen Danube in March of that year. The horde split into three spearheads, and one, led by the khan himself, made for the capital. The Long Wall from Selymbria (modern Sili-vri) on the Sea of Marmora to the Black Sea, which the emperor Anastasius had built as a "distant early warning" defense for the capital, was in disrepair and there were no troops: in desperation Justinian dispatched the ornamental Scholarians to defend the Long Wall, but they proved entirely ineffectual, as might have been expected. At this moment of crisis, Justinian summoned Belisarius from retirement, and the old field marshal laid an ambush for the Kutrigurs and routed them.

Then Justinian took the credit for the victory. He recalled Belisarius and himself went out to Selymbria to oversee the reconstruction of the Long Wall. Once the job was finished, Justinian made a ceremonial reentry into the city. His route took him through the Charisius Gate, along the northern branch of the Mese, and past the Church of the Holy Apostles. Eleven years before, Theodora's funeral cortege had wound its way there from the imperial palace, and her mortal remains had been laid to rest in her sarcophagus of Sardian stone within the mausoleum Justinian had built for himself and his empress. Now Justinian halted his triumphal procession, entered the mausoleum where he knelt before Theodora's tomb, and lit votive candles for the repose of her soul. He had not forgotten his old ally.[16] The partnership of Justinian and Theodora was one of the great love affairs of history.

Apart from a couple of battered sculptured portraits that may be hers, the only portrait of her that survives is in the church of San Vitale in Ravenna, built with funds from a local banker, Julius Argentarius.[17] It was dedicated the year before Theodora's death. One side of the chancel has a mosaic of Justinian and his retinue. Facing it on the other side is a mosaic of Theodora and her entourage; the woman on her left has been identified tentatively as Antonina. Theodora's great eyes gaze out from beneath an elaborate pearl diadem that seems almost to overwhelm, and her face is noticeably thinner than those of her attendants. With a little imagination, we may detect a fragility that hints, perhaps, at the inexorable progress of the cancer that was soon to kill her. But she was no weak woman. She left an imprint on society because her contemporaries believed that she wielded independent power in a man's world, where feminine power was usually limited. Her authority depended on Justinian, and yet by force of her own personality and the respect that Justinian had for her, she could act with a degree of independence. She inspired either love or hate. No one could deal with her memory and remain neutral.

She had fought a good fight, though she left the course unfinished.

The Peerless Empress

Women were never without power in the ancient Mediterranean world. Given that life was, by modern standards, brief and nasty for most people, whatever their gender, and that society demanded that a female's primary function was to perpetuate the species, women belonging to the ruling elite exerted a remarkable degree of authority. Not, perhaps, in democratic Athens of the fifth century B.C.: the wife of Pericles is at best a shadowy figure, though his mistress, Aspasia, was popularly believed to exercise too much influence. But even in classical Athens where respectable women did not meddle openly in public affairs, two comedies of Aristophanes, the *Women in the Assembly* and the *Lysistrata*, show an awareness of a feminine agenda that differed from its male counterpart and imagined situations in which women could impose their policies on the state.

But the status of women in classical Athens was not typical in the Mediterranean world. Women in Sparta never shared the lifestyle of their Athenian counterparts, and the women of ancient Macedon were comparatively liberated. The courts of the Hellenistic world where Macedonian dynasties ruled produced a remarkable clutch of powerful princesses, and it is in these royal households that we find the earliest paradigms of the Byzantine empresses: women who took up the reins of power whenever, for some reason, male authority was enfeebled. The Ptolemaic dynasty in Egypt yielded a remarkable crop of dominant Cleopatras. Cleopatra I (ca. 215–176 B.C.) ruled as regent for her young son Ptolemy VI. Cleopatra II was a formidable lady who was first co-regent with her brother and husband, Ptolemy VI, and another brother, Ptolemy VIII Euergetes, and after her husband/brother's death, fought for power with Euergetes for almost twenty years until she forced him to accept her as partner. Cleopatra III was a turbulent woman who incited two rebellions, neither successful, but nonetheless she managed to put her second son on the throne of Egypt as Ptolemy X, who found his mother a troublesome champion once he was king and disposed of her. Cleopatra VII had affairs with Julius Caesar and Mark Antony and made an audacious bid for imperial power in Rome. She left a mark on history such as few royal dynasts have done.

The Augustas who partnered Rome's early emperors were equally adept, though they generally followed a different model more in keeping with Roman traditions. Livia, the last wife of the emperor Augustus, might have served as an example for Theodora if she needed one or was familiar with the history of Rome a half millennium before her time, neither of which is likely. Livia's family connections were impeccable: she belonged to the old, distinguished family of the Livii, and her first husband, the father of her sons, was a scion of the Claudian *gens*, whose antecedents went back to the earliest days of Rome. Like Theodora, she had no children by the emperor. Like her, too, she belonged to the inner circle of imperial counselors, and Augustus valued her advice. But she was a lady with background, born into the ruling elite, which in the early years of the principate, Augustus could not afford to ignore. She brought influence, contacts, and social standing to the Julio-Claudian dynasty. A parvenue like Theodora could never have shared the throne with Augustus. Even the popular emperor Titus (A.D. 79–81), once he succeeded his father Vespasian to the throne, thought it wise to give up his Jewish Berenice, though she belonged to the Herodian royal house from Judaea. She was too un-Roman.

Yet as empress, Livia cultivated the persona of a respectable Roman matron. The paradigm was still Lucretia, the honorable wife of Roman tradition, whose rape by Sextus Tarquinius sparked the uprising that drove the Tarquin kings from Rome, and though the early empire could produce forceful Italian empresses who wielded power behind the scenes, the eastern Mediterranean did better. The women of the Severan dynasty in the early third century—Julia Domna, the Syrian wife of Septimius Severus, her sister Julia Maesa, and Maesa's daughter, Julia Mamaea, the mother of the emperor Severus Alexander, sprung from the priestly dynasty of Emesa—reached new levels of feminine influence. But their authority was greatest when male power faltered. Severus Alexander was young and Mamaea found him pliable. After his death came turmoil, by the middle of the century anarchy, and by its end the empire was moving into a new space under Diocletian's new dispensation. With the dedication of the new capital of Constantinople in 330, the Christian empire began. The legal status of women changed very little, but Christianity conveyed a shift in attitude that brought them greater respect. The Christian church welcomed both male and female saints. Women of all classes, as well as men, could dispute theology and in the process discover that they had minds and could form opinions that were worth something.

Yet it remained true that the influence of imperial women was greatest when male power was weak. When the emperor Valens perished in the calamitous defeat at Adrianople in 368, his widow, Domnica Augusta, organized the defense of Constantinople and provided direction in the crucial period between the defeat and the appointment of the emperor Theodosius I.[18] Her brief supremacy bridged the gap between two male regimes. But in the two centuries that followed the death of Theodosius in 395, when emperors no longer led their armies in the field but stayed in their palaces in Constantinople, or in Ravenna as long as there was a western emperor, women had a greater opportunity to exercise power in the center of operations than they had had since the time of the Severan dynasty. When Theodosius I died, the masculine energy of his house died with him. His sons, Honorius, emperor in the West, and Arcadius, emperor in the East, were men of limited ability, and the last male of the dynasty, Arcadius' son, Theodosius II, was easily led. But at the same time, the imperial house produced a remarkable crop of dominant women. Powerful women and weak emperors went together.

Arcadius' wife, Eudoxia, the daughter of a Frankish general, was chosen for him by a palace eunuch. Arcadius himself was a torpid prince; Synesius of Cyrene[19] likened him to a "jellyfish" in a speech that was intended for delivery before the emperor and his courtiers, though we may doubt if he had the hardihood actually to deliver it. But Arcadius filled his role as imperial stud well enough and Eudoxia was correspondingly fertile: she bore four daughters and a son between 397 and 403, and in the following year she died of a miscarriage. Her fecundity was a significant element of her power; as wife of an emperor and mother of a royal family that included a future emperor, she had a right to the imperial demeanor she assumed, and she possessed the vigor her husband lacked. After her coronation as Augusta in 400, her effigy appears on gold, silver, and bronze coins from the mints of Constantinople and elsewhere in the East, an honor that Theodora never enjoyed. Her coin portraits show a disembodied arm reaching down to crown her. It is the "Right Hand of God," and the symbolism, which was borrowed from Jewish art, was unmistakable. Her clash with the handpicked patriarch of Constantinople, John Chrysostom, was a battle between a male chauvinist and misogynist to boot and a dominant female who would not assume the submissive role Chrysostom considered proper for a woman. Chrysostom went into exile in 404, and before the year was out, Eudoxia herself died in childbirth, still fulfilling the reproductive role that she could not escape. But she had won the contest. In the struggle between church and state, it was she more than her husband, the emperor, who exercised imperial power.

Eudoxia's daughter, Pulcheria, was a worthy successor to her mother. Theodosius II was only seven years old when Arcadius died, and the administration was in the able hands of the praetorian prefect Anthemius, but it was Pulcheria who oversaw the education of the young emperor. When she was fourteen she decided to remain a virgin and extended her decision to her sisters. Like the virginity of Queen Elizabeth I, it had political consequences; it protected Theodosius II from the imperial ambitions of any possible brother-in-law. In 414, the year that Anthemius disappeared from office, Theodosius proclaimed Pulcheria Augusta, and like her mother before her, her portraits appear on the coins. She was now the power behind the throne.

In 420-21 Theodosius married a woman from Athens, whose father was a Neoplatonic philosopher and had named his daughter Athenais, but when she came to Constantinople, her father having (perhaps?) died, she embraced Christianity and was baptized Eudocia. The new empress, and, after 423, Augusta, and her party at court soon challenged Pulcheria's control of her brother. She eclipsed Pulcheria after the first Council of Ephesus (431) that condemned Nestorius for his extreme Diphysitism, and after a quarrel, Pulcheria made a temporary retreat from government. In 438 Eudocia departed from the court for the Holy Land, accompanied by Saint Melania the Younger who had made a visitation to Constantinople and was returning to her nunnery on the Mount of Olives. In early 439 she made a dramatic return, bringing with her the relics of the first martyr, Saint Stephen. Once back in court, she allied herself with the able and wily eunuch Chrysaphius Tzumas, who used her to break Pulcheria's power and then brought down Eudocia herself.

John Malalas recounts a story that Theodosius gave his wife a remarkable apple of great size that a poor man had given him, and she in turn gave it to a handsome young courtier who, not knowing its origin, gave it to Theodosius. Apples were love tokens, and Theodosius ordered the courtier put to death. The story sounds like a folktale, but whether it is true or not, Chrysaphius did use suspicion of adultery to bring down Eudocia. The weak-willed emperor was persuaded to believe the allegation. Eudocia quit the capital again for Jerusalem, and this time she did not return, although she kept her title of "Augusta" and did not abandon her interest in church politics. The Monophysites were to remember her fondly.

As for Pulcheria, when Theodosius died, she returned swiftly from the fringes of power. She chose the next emperor. She did not have a free hand, for Aspar the generalissimo (*magister utriusque militiae*) controlled the army and Pulcheria's choice was Aspar's *domesticus,* Marcian. But to the populace of Constantinople, Pulcheria represented legitimacy: she gave Marcian the diadem, and she married him, though she kept her virginity intact. Chrysaphius was executed, and the Council of Chalcedon reversed the verdict of the Council of Ephesus two years before, which had supported the Monophysite teachings of Chrysaphius' godfather, Eutyches. History repeated itself when the emperor Zeno died. His widow, Ariadne, the daughter of the emperor Leo, chose Anastasius as the next emperor and the populace respected her choice. She represented continuity.

When Justinian died, his successor was Justin II and his empress was Theodora's niece, Sophia, a forceful, ambitious woman who had an opportunity to exercise imperial power such as her aunt never possessed. She was likely the daughter of Theodora's sister, the old burlesque star Comito whom Theodora had attended on stage when she made her own acting debut, and if so, her father was probably the young Armenian officer Sittas who had been killed in a skirmish in Armenia during the interval of the short-lived "Endless Peace" with Persia (532–40).[20] Sophia was only one generation removed from the theater, but a single generation was enough to ennoble a family. Sophia, like Theodora, was her husband's partner, and unlike Theodora, her partnership was acknowledged on Justin's coinage. When Justin went mad during the disastrous war he provoked with Persia, which resulted in the loss of the great border fortress of Daras, Sophia stepped into the breach. She sent a letter to Khusru, appealing to his chivalry, and made first a one-year truce and then managed to extend it to three years.

The senate consulted her on the succession, and in 574 she persuaded Justin to adopt as his son and heir the commander of the Excubitors, Tiberius, and to make him co-emperor four years later. She hoped to marry him when Justin died, though she must have known that he was already married, and she persuaded the patriarch to suggest the union to Tiberius, but here she miscalculated: Tiberius was quite unwilling to abandon his wife, Ino, who took the name Anastasia when she became empress.[21] Sophia, however, had no intention of yielding place to Ino. She clung to her status stubbornly. She refused to move from her quarters in the palace and forced Tiberius to yield; he had to build an extension on the northern side of the palace for his own use. Sophia was consulted again by the senate when Tiberius was on his deathbed, and she selected Maurice, an experienced general and a good choice.[22] She was a dominant woman who would not be left on the sidelines, but her authority rested not merely on her forceful character and political skill. Clearly her ability also made a deep impression on contemporaries.

These empresses were dominant women who knew how to wield power at court. Yet all of them, even Athenais, the maid from Athens who became the wife of Theodosius II, began their careers with some power base. Theodora began hers with none. Actresses were the outcasts of society. She was a woman without connections or education, but she seems to have been able to hold her own among an elite that valued a classical education. We assume that she was literate, but there must have been many women in the theater who were not, and we know nothing of Theodora's schooling. Yet as empress she could greet and chat with two popes as well as emissaries from Rome, and papal legates were by no means always competent in Greek. Could Theodora speak Latin as well as Greek? Justinian was bilingual, but what of Theodora? Probably she picked up a smattering of Latin, but we cannot assume any great familiarity. Could she speak Syriac? She had friends and protégés who could, including John of Ephesus and Jacob Bara'dai, and after Hecebolus discarded her, her wanderings had brought her to Antioch, where she may have heard sermons in Syriac and possibly comprehended them. Constantinople was a polyglot city where an alumna of the streets might have picked up a working knowledge of several languages.

She was no great theologian, but she knew the basics, and her expertise was sufficient to earn Justinian's respect. She reached her position because she was able to capture Justinian's love and keep it; and with her quick intelligence, she learned quickly how to maneuver her way through the intrigues of the court. As empress she looked after the interests of her extended family and her friends and thereby created a power base for herself. But so did everyone else in positions of authority. She built up her own clientage drawn both from the Monophysite hierarchy and from the imperial service, and she had her own circle of informants. She could be ruthless, and her enemies knew it.

There was a second difference. Other women exercised authority most effectively when male power faltered. Except for a brief few weeks when Justinian caught the plague, he was in charge. Theodora was the partner of one of the ablest emperors in Byzantine history. If he consulted her, it was because he valued her advice. In this respect, his relationship with her is analogous to that of the emperor Augustus and Livia. Procopius of Caesarea claimed that her attraction for Justinian was sexual, and Theodora was already an experienced bed partner when Justinian married her, skilled at titillating a middle-aged man. Justinian hoped for an heir, and Theodora would have liked nothing better than to fulfill the maternal role that was expected of women. Yet long after it was clear that she could not bear him a child, Justinian remained faithful. Lust may have drawn Justinian to her at the start, but it was her intelligence that kept him faithful. When she was dead, Justinian missed her companionship and her loyalty, but most of all he missed her nous.

It is a coincidence that illustrates the power imperial women could wield in Byzantium that the two most important developments in the rift between Orthodoxy and Monophysitism were the work of women. Pulcheria was responsible for the Council of Chalcedon, which produced the Chalcedonian Creed, the rock on which all later efforts to heal the breach foundered. Theodora made the rise of a Monophysite clergy possible and became the god-mother of the Monophysite churches. Yet Theodora differed from her imperial sisters in one significant way. None had exercised so much influence as Theodora while male authority was intact, or for that matter, completely in charge. And none had started so low and risen to the top as she did.

When Theodora was on her deathbed, she entreated Justinian to promise that he would care for her Monophysite refugees whom she sheltered in the Palace of Hormisdas. Her appeal betrayed her apprehension. She knew what her power base was. The Chalcedonians represented the ascendancy in Constantinople. Theodora's family was nouveau riche, and its fortune depended entirely on her. As soon as she was dead, her enemies would move in, and only Justinian could keep them at bay.

It is interesting to speculate what might have happened if she had outlived Justinian. Suppose bubonic plague had killed him in 542, which must have seemed not unlikely for a few weeks. Then, like her niece Sophia, Theodora would probably have yielded power unwillingly. But in the end she would have lost it even more completely than Sophia. For the likely successor of Justinian was his cousin, Germanus, and Theodora recognized him as her enemy and a threat to the status of her family.

Abbreviations

Bury, *LRE*	J. B. Bury, *History of the Later Roman Empire*. I–II. London, 1923. Rpt. New York, 1958.
DHP	*Dictionnaire Historique de la Papauté*. Paris, 1994.
CathEnc.	*Catholic Encyclopedia*. New York, 1907.
CE	*Coptic Encyclopedia*. New York, 1991.
CSCO	Corpus scriptorum christianorum orientalum.
DHGE	*Dictionnaire d'histoire et de géographie ecclésiastique*. Paris, 1967–.
Dict. de Spir.	*Dictionnaire de spiritualité*. Paris, 1982.
EGHT	*Encyclopedia of Greece and the Hellenic Tradition*, ed. Graham Speake. London/Chicago, 2000.
EncycRel	*The Encyclopedia of Religion*, ed. Mircea Eliade. New York, 1995.
Hastings' Encyclopedia	James Hastings, ed., *Encyclopaedia of Religion and Ethics*. Edinburgh/New York, 1916–17.
Jones, *LRE*	A. H. M. Jones, *The Later Roman Empire, 284–602*. I–II. Oxford, 1964.
Late Antiquity	*Late Antiquity: A Guide to the Postclassical World*, edd. G. W. Bowersock, Peter Brown, Oleg Grabar. Cambridge, Mass./London, 1999.
LCL	*Loeb Classical Library*. Cambridge, Mass./London.
NCE	*New Catholic Encyclopedia*. New York, 1967.
ODB	*Oxford Dictionary of Byzantium*. New York/Oxford, 1991.
PLRE	*The Prosopography of the Later Roman Empire*, I, (A.D. 260–395), edd. A. H. M. Jones, J. R. Martindale, J. Morris. Cambridge, 1971. II, (A.D. 395–527), ed. J. R. Martindale, 1980. IIIA and IIIB (A.D. 527–641), ed. J. R. Martindale. Cambridge, 1992.
PO	*Patrologia orientalis*, edd. R. Graffin, F. Nau. I. Paris, 1904.
RE	*Paulys Realenzyklopädie der classischen Altertumswissenschaft*.

Notes

Preface

1. Diehl (1904).
2. Bridge (1978).

Introduction

1. The *ODB* cites the editions of these authors mentioned here. Some have appeared (or will soon appear) in the series Translated Texts for Historians published by the University of Liverpool Press.

2. Cf. Evans (1996b).

3. 1.11.8.

4. *Anek.* 6.22–23.

5. *Late Antiquity*, s.v. "Anicia Juliana" (Charles Pazdernik); *ODB*, s.v. "Anicia Juliana" (W. W. Kaegi).

6. Cf. Treadgold (1997), pp. 196–98.

7. Cf. Witakowski (1987), pp. 83–84.

8. Cf. Harvey (1990).

9. Zachariah of Mytilene, who lived long enough to attend the Church Council of Constantinople in 536, wrote a *Church History* in Greek for the years 450–91, which survives as a Syriac epitome forming Bks. 3–6 in a chronicle compiled by an unknown monk at Amida in 569. See *ODB*, s.v. "Zacharias of Mytilene" (B. Baldwin and S. H. Griffith).

10. 3.69.2–3; cf. Pazdernik (1994), p. 262.

11. Cf. Croke (1990); Scott (1990); *EGHT*, s.v. "Chronicle" (Elizabeth M. Jeffreys).

12. Diehl (1904).

13. Browning (1971), p. 257.

14. Cf. Lemerle (1964), p. 58: "[T]he empress Theodora was not, like the emperor, dazzled by the mirage of the West. She knew that the empire was, in the last analysis, a thing of the East." The evidence to support such a view is scanty.

Chapter 1. A New Dynasty Takes Power

1. *Nov.* 80.

2. *Anek.* 19.7; cf. Carney (1971), p. 101, n. 1, for skepticism.

3. Cf. Greatrex (1998), who treats the years 502-32 as a single period of war, interrupted by an uneasy peace from 506 to 527.

4. Evans (1996a), pp. 222-24.

5. On Hypatius, see Greatrex (1996).

6. *PLRE* II, s.v. "Aelia Augusta."

7. *Anek.* 6.15-18; 8.3.

8. Constantine Porphyrogenitus, *De Caer.* I. 94.431; Malalas, 17.2 (p. 411); Evagrius *HE* 4.2. See also Vasiliev (1950), pp. 69-82; Boak (1919), pp. 39-41; Evans (1996a), pp. 11-12.

9. *Anek.* 6.26; Marcellinus *sub anno* 519; *Chron. Pasch.* 519 (pp. 611-12: Bonn ed.), cf. Vasiliev (1950), pp. 107-8.

10. *De Mag.* 3.51.5. Marinus reappears briefly as praetorian prefect in 519: see Greatrex (1996), p. 129.

11. *Anek.* 6. 1-17. Evagrius *HE* 4.1 identifies Justin as a "Thracian" and the name of Justinian's father, "Sabbatius," is Thracian: Vasiliev (1950), p. 60. See *PLRE* II, s.v. "Iustinus 4," for references.

12. *Anek.* 6.17, cf. *PLRE* II, s.v. "Lupicina *quae et* Euphemia 5.

13. Theophanes A.M. 6011.

14. The *Chronicle of Pseudo-Dionysius of Tel-Mahre* (*ann.* 829) credits Euphemia for Justin's sharp break with Anastasius' policy of favoring Monophysitism.

15. Chadwick (1967), pp. 200-10.

16. Frend (1976), pp. 80-81.

17. John of Antioch, frg. 214c; cf. Greatrex (1996), p. 135.

18. Malalas 16.16 (pp. 403-5).

19. The other Master of the Soldiers in the Presence was Justinian. Another of Justin's nephews, Germanus, replaced Vitalian in the office of Master of the Soldiers in Thrace, where he soon established his military reputation by winning a victory over a group of Slavic raiders: see Treadgold (1997), pp. 175-76.

20. Michael the Syrian, *Chron.* 9.13.

21. Bakker (1985). The excavator, Michael Gough, to the best of my knowledge, never connected the desertion of Alahan with the persecution of the Monophysites under Justin I, but the monastery was almost certainly Monophysite and the date would seem to fit. See Evans (1999), p. 142.

22. *Anek.* 6.27-28; Evagrius *HE* 4.3. See *PLRE* II, s.v. "Fl. Vitalianus 2." On Justin's religious policy, see Vasiliev (1950), pp. 132-253.

23. See Evans (1996a), pp. 34-40.

24. *Anek.* 7.33.

25. Harrison (1986), pp. 8-9. Anicia Juliana was the daughter of Olybrius, a short-lived western emperor in 472, and Placidia the younger, the daughter of Valentinian III.

26. *Anek.* 7.1–38; 9.35–46; see Diehl (1904), pp. 30–31; Greatrex (1997), p. 66. Malalas 17.12 (p. 416) tells a different story, though it seems to be based on the same incident. It relates that Justin appointed a former Count of the Orient, Theodotos, as urban prefect, with orders to suppress street violence, but when Theodotos executed a wealthy senator of the rank of *illustris* without consulting the emperor, he was exiled. Thereupon Theodore was appointed. Malalas gives Theodore the sobriquet "Teganistes" (the "fryer") rather than "Kolokynthios," but they may be the same person. The *Anekdota* should not necessarily be preferred over Malalas.

27. Malalas 17.18 (p. 422).

28. *Anek.* 7.3; 10.19; cf. Browning (1971), pp. 64–65; Evans (1996a), pp. 38–40. The Blues and Greens had no consistent religious or political policies, but historians ever since Baronius have suspected that the Blues were champions of Chalcedonian orthodoxy. Edward Gibbon thought that the Greens harbored a "secret attachment to the family or sect of Anastasius," that is, Monophysitism, whereas the Blues supported Justinian and orthodoxy: see Bury (1908), IV, pp. 220–22, esp. n. 45. The family of Anastasius remained powerful in Constantinople until the Nika revolt of 532, but on the question of theological orthodoxy, even it was divided: see Cameron (1978). Cameron's view is that the Blue and Green parties never had any consistent theological policies: see Cameron (1974).

29. Cf. Browning (1971), p. 64.

Chapter 2. The Early Life of Theodora

1. Nicephorus Callistus *HE* 17.28. Nicephorus was patriarch of Constantinople from 806 to 815.

2. See Storrs and O'Brien (1930), p. 49.

3. More correctly "Justinianopolis": see Hill (1940), pp. 228–90.

4. No source mentions a brother. However, the empress Sophia, wife of Justinian's successor, Justin II, was Theodora's niece, and Stein (1949), p. 744, n. 4, points out that John of Ephesus seems to have thought the relationship was through Sophia's father and not her mother.

5. John Lyd., *De Mag.* 1.40.3; cf. *Late Antiquity*, s.v. "Actors and Acting" (Richard Miles).

6. *Homily* 7.6–7; cf. Traversari (1960), pp. 45–46.

7. *Novel.* 105.1.

8. *CodTheod.* 15.7.1. (A.D. 371). See the comments of Cameron (1976), pp. 80–82, on the social standing of theater personnel.

9. Choricius of Gaza 32.114–17 (*In Defense of Mimes*) makes this point: even if the party whose charioteer won continued to cheer after the mime started, the losing side would be distracted by the mime and less likely to take offense. On Choricius, see *EGHT,* s.v. "Choricius of Gaza" (George F. Karamanolis).

10. *CodTheod.* 15.7.8 (A.D. 381). See Cottas (1931), pp. 51–52. Women did not attend the theater: Fisher (1978), p. 258, citing Procopius, *Wars* 1.24.6.

11. *Anek.* 9.8–26.

12. See Clark (1993), pp. 29–31, on the prevailing morality of the stage.

13. *Anek.* 9.22.

14. *Anek.* 9.16.

15. Diehl (1901), pp. 41–46.

16. *Anek.* 9.25–26.

17. Norwich (1990), pp. 192–93.

18. *Anek.* 17.16–23.

19. *PLRE* II, s.v. "Hecebolus." The manuscripts of the *Anekdota* give two spellings of his name: "Hekebolus" at 9.27 and "Hekebolius" at 12.30.

20. *CodTheod.* 15.7.5 (380) prescribes a fine of five gold pounds for abducting an actress, but it is unlikely that the law was enforced at this time, if ever.

21. Houssaye (1885), p. 578, suggests that Theodora's reputation had preceded her to Libya.

22. PO I, p. 459.

23. John of Nikiu 514. Cf. Rubin (1960), p. 104; Hardy (1968), p. 31.

24. Dawes and Baynes (1948), p. 88. Note also Evagrius' complaint (*HE* 4.30) that if a prostitute informed against someone, charging him with a crime, then he would be found guilty, legal rights notwithstanding, and she and Justinian would share the victim's wealth.

25. *Anek.* 12.28–32.

26. *Anek.* 9.30.

27. *Patria* 3.93 (ed. Preger, p. 248); cf. Nagl, *RE*, s.v. "Theodora," col. 1777. Holmes (1912) uses this tradition for a legend of his own: that on her way back from Antioch to Constantinople she found herself in Paphlagonia, where the population was puritanical and theater avoided, and it was there that she abandoned her wicked past.

28. Procopius, *De Aed.* 1.9.11, reports that Justinian replaced the martyrion of Saint Panteleëmon with a magnificent church but does not mention Theodora. Clearly contemporaries knew nothing about Theodora's humble house at the martyrion. Cf. Rubin (1960), pp. 104–5.

29. Michael the Syrian, *Chron.* 9.20; *Chronicle of 819:* CSCO 81, p. 192.

30. *Certain Saints and Servants of God, Thomas, and Stephen and Zwt'.*

31. PO 17, p. 189. Bury, *LRE* II, p. 28, n. 5, believed that the words "from the brothel" which are in Greek, inserted into the Syriac text, must be an interpolation, for John, who admired Theodora, would never have written anything so unflattering. However, twentieth-century prudery is out of place here, as Vasiliev (1950), p. 97, remarks. Nonetheless, Theodora's origins fueled the disdain that the ruling elite of the capital felt for Theodora.

32. Cf. Harvey (1990), p. 40.

33. Av. Cameron (1985), p. 77, also cites as corroboration the eighth-century *Parastaseis Syntomoi Chronikai*, which mentions an empress, unnamed but very likely Theodora, as "formerly shameless but later chaste."

34. I infer this date from *CodJust.* 5.4.23: see n. 78, below.

35. *CodJust.* 5.4.23, undated but addressed to the praetorian prefect Demosthenes,

who was appointed in 520-21 and continued in office until 524, which thus gives a *terminus ante quem* for the law and for Euphemia's death: *PLRE* II, s.v. "Fl. Theodorus Petrus Demosthenes 4." See Diehl (1904), pp. 53-54; Vasiliev (1950), pp. 392-97; Rubin (1960), p. 187; Stein (1949), p. 236.

36. *Anek.* 9.51. Daube (1967), p. 392, notes that the law did not cover prostitutes but only former actresses.

37. Cameron (1978), pp. 271-72. On Theodora's skillful maneuvering of her family into the upper reaches of society, see Av. Cameron (1985), pp. 80-81.

38. Gerostorgios (1982), p. 33, dates the marriage to 526, citing Zonaras 14.5. However, this would imply a two-year wait and probably longer between the promulgation of the law legalizing the marriage and the wedding itself.

39. See above, n. 6.

40. Boak (1919), p. 41; Evans (1996a), p. 112; Vasiliev (1950), pp. 100-1; Browning (1971), p. 69. For the date of the ceremony in the Triclinium, see *Anek.* 9.53. Zonaras 14.5D indicates that Justinian and Theodora each received an acclamation.

41. *Anek.* 10.6-10.

42. *Nov.* 8.1.

43. Nagl, *RE*, s.v. "Theodora 11," col. 1779; cf. A. G. Gibson, *NCE*, s.v. "Theodora, Byzantine Empress (1)."

44. *Anek.* 17.32-36. Mime artists wore their hair long, and their stage names frequently referred to their hair. "Chrysomallo" means "golden-haired." See Cottas (1931), p. 42.

45. *Anek.* 15.24-35.

46. *Anek.* 30.21-26. Cf. Stein (1949), pp. 237-39.

47. *Anek.* 30.21; cf. Av. Cameron (1981), pp. 208-11.

48. Marcellinus, *sub anno* 528.

49. Mango (1972a), p. 104, n. 239.

50. *Anek.* 10.11. Cf. *De Aed.* 1.11.8.

51. *Anek.* 14. 6-9; 15.36-38; 22.26-28.

52. *Anek.* 14.7-8.

53. *Anek.* 10.5.

54. *HE* 4.9.

55. "Aphthartodoketism," which carried Monophysite theology to its logical conclusion and denied the human nature of Christ to such a degree that it argued that his body escaped corruption after death.

Chapter 3. The Early Years in Power

1. Evans (1996a), pp. 132-33.

2. Zonaras 14.6.

3. *Nov.* 8.1.

4. *Anek.* 30.24.

5. Norwich (1990), p. 194.

6. *De Aed.* 1.11.9.

7. Mango (1972b), p. 190. One of the lost sections of John Lydus' *De Magistratibus* had the heading, "On the pious empress Theodora and how she benefited the public good"; Pazdernik (1994), p. 262, n. 33. The inscription on the architrave beneath the dome of Saints Sergius and Bacchus reads in full: "Other sovereigns gave honored dead men whose labor was unprofitable, but our sceptered Justinian, fostering piety, honors with a splendid abode Sergius the Servant of Christ, Begetter of all things, whom not the burning breath of fire, nor the sword, nor any other constraint of torments disturbed; but who endured to be slain for the sake of Christ God, gaining by his blood heaven as his home. May he in all things guard the rule of the sleepless sovereign and increase the power of the God-crowned Theodora whose mind is adorned with piety, whose constant toil lies in unsparing efforts to nourish the destitute." Quoted from Fowden (1999), p. 130. The dedication names only Saint Sergius, whose cult had become particularly popular in Syria and Mesopotamia, and it seems that Justinian dedicated the church to him alone. But the ascription to Saint Bacchus as well goes back to Justinian's reign: cf. Procopius *De Aed.* 1.4.3. On the cult of Saint Sergius, see Fowden (1999).

8. Procopius, *De Aed.* 1.4.7. For the date: George Cedrenus *A.M. 6021* (I, pp. 642–63: Bonn ed.); cf. Matthews (1971), pp. 47–51, who points out with justice that Cedrenus is not a highly reliable source.

9. *HE* 4.10.

10. Henry (1967), pp. 305–6; Downey (1968), passim. On the deacon of Hagia Sophia, see *ODB*, s.v. "Agapetus."

11. *Anek.* 9.31–32.

12. *CodJust.* 7.37.3; cf. Coleman-Norton (1966), p. 1116; Diehl (1901), p. 61.

13. Quoted from Coleman-Norton (1966), p. 1116.

14. *Anek.* 15.6–9.

15. *Anek.* 15.36–38.

16. *De Aed.* 5.3.16–20; cf. Moorhead (1994), p. 31. For the date: Mango and Scott (1997), p. 286, n. 2.

17. John of Ephesus, *Third Part of the Ecclesiastical History* 1.30–31.

18. Evagrius *HE* 4.28 reports that the cross was a joint gift of Theodora and Justinian; at 6.21 he reports it as Theodora's alone. For its theft, see Theophanes, *Chron.* 5.13.1–2.

19. Malalas 17.19, 22 (p. 423).

20. Malalas 18.24 (pp. 440–41); John of Nikiu, 93.3.

21. Cf. *Anthol. Graec.* 16.77, 78, 80, 277, 278, 283.

22. Evagrius, *HE* 4.34.

23. *Anek.* 17.5–6.

24. *De Aed.* 1.9.1–10, cf. Janin (1964), p. 151. The convent was still standing in the eleventh century.

25. 18.24 (pp. 440–41).

26. *CodTheod.* 15.8.2 (A.D. 428); cf. Clark (1993), p. 30.

27. *CodJust.* 11.41.7 (ca. AD 460). See in general Jones, *LRE*, p. 976.

28. *Nov.* 14 (Schoell); cf. Debidour (1877), p. 19; Jones, *LRE*, p. 976; Clark (1993), pp. 29–31.

29. *Wars* 7.31.14.

30. Procopius, *Wars* 7.31.17–18; 7.32.18. For Theodora's hostility to Germanus, see *Anek.* 5.8.

31. *Wars* 7.31.1–16; cf. Evans (1996a), p. 170.

32. *PLRE* IIIA, s.v. "Artabanes 2."

33. *De Aed.* 1.2.17.

34. Krautheimer (1965), pp. 175–77.

35. Forsyth (1968), p. 9.

36. Malalas, 17.19 (p. 423); cf. Evans (1996a), p. 226.

37. Zonaras 14.7.B–C; followed by Diehl (1904), pp. 242–45.

38. *De Aed.* 1.4.9–24.

39. Rice (1954), pp. 70–71; 79; Bury, *LRE* II, pp. 53–54. Rice, who considers the mosaics Justinianic, suggests that these were the first full series of doctrinal mosaics of a narrative character that decorated a church in Constantinople and compares them with those in S. Apollinare Nuovo in Ravenna. It is perhaps more likely that they date from the restoration of the church by the emperor Basil I after the Iconoclast period. See *ODB*, s.v. "Holy Apostles, Church of the."

40. *Nov.* 8.1.

41. *CodJust.* 1.4.33.

42. *Nov.* 51.

43. *CodJust.* 5.4.23 (pp. 520–24).

44. *CodJust.* 1.4.33.

45. *Nov.* 51.

46. *Nov.* 117.4 (A.D. 541); cf. Debidour (1877), pp. 17–18.

47. *Nov.* 5.2; cf. Evans (1996a), pp. 209–10.

48. *Anek.* 17.32–37.

49. *Anek.* 17.24–26.

Chapter 4. The Nika Revolt

1. The chief ancient sources are Procopius, *Wars* 1.24.1–25; Malalas 18.71 (pp. 473–76); *Chron. Pasch.*, pp. 620–28; Theophanes A.M. 6024; Ps. Zachariah of Mitylene 9.14. For modern studies, see Bury (1897); Greatrex (1997).

2. Malalas 17.18 (p. 422: Bonn ed.); Stein (1949), p. 240; cf. Greatrex (1997), pp. 66–67.

3. Malalas 18.41 (p. 448: Bonn ed.); Stein (1949), p. 449.

4. Evagrius *HE* 4.32.

5. *Anek.* 10.19–11.4.

6. Malalas 17.18 (p. 422) records that as soon as Justinian became co-emperor he sent a rescript to every city ordering rioters and murderers to be punished, regardless of their party. See Greatrex (1997), p. 65, n. 32.

7. For *Akta*, which were protocols of councils or assemblies kept by a secretarial staff, see *Late Antiquity*, s.v. "Acta" (Denis Feissel). The *Akta dia Kalapodion* were preserved in

full by Theophanes A.M. 6024 and in part by the *Chron. Pasch.*, p. 620 (Bonn ed.). The most recent translation is in Mango and Scott, trans., *The Chronicle of Theophanes Confessor*, pp. 277–79. See also the discussion of M. Whitby and M. Whitby in their translation of the *Chronicon Paschale* in the Liverpool Translated Texts series (1989), pp. 113–14. Karagiannopoulos (1995), p. 429, makes the plausible suggestion that the unsatisfactory (from the viewpoint of the Greens) encounter with Justinian recorded in the *Akta* led to more street violence, which the imperial authorities attempted to suppress with an even hand, thereby alienating both parties.

8. See *PLRE* IIIA: "Calopodius 1." He is otherwise unknown. The *Chronicon Paschale* calls him *spatharocubicularius,* which Whitby and Whitby translate as "*cubicularius* and *spatharius*" (p. 114, n. 345). His replacement as *spatharius,* Narses, a protégé of Theodora, held the office during the Nika riot, which is, perhaps, an argument for dating this dialogue at least a few days before the outbreak, for unless the two held the office simultaneously, which seems unlikely, Calopodius must have been replaced between the time that the *Akta* were chanted in the Hippodrome and the Nika riot. The easiest solution is that Calopodius (= "the man with lovely feet") was a sobriquet for Narses. This suggestion was made by Karlin-Hayter (1973), pp. 87–88, and is attractive but cannot be proved.

Bury (1897), p. 118, followed by Evans (1996a), p. 119, dated the *Akta* to Sunday, 11 January, but as Stein (1949), p. 450, n. 1, points out, no games would be held on Sunday. Thus he dates the dialogue to Saturday, 10 January. But that would put the *Akta* and the executions of the felons on the same day. There is a serious objection to this: the *Akta* show the emperor's overt partiality, whereas the urban prefect's action shows that imperial policy had changed to one of neutrality and arrests had been made of both Green and Blue malefactors. One solution is to disconnect the *Akta* from the Nika revolt entirely: see discussion of Greatrex (1997), p. 68, n. 41. The other is to follow Karagiannopoulos (1995), p. 429, and allow enough time between the *Akta* and the riot, first for renewed street violence, then a change of policy to impartial justice to counter the violence, which led to the arrest of both Blue and Green troublemakers by the urban prefect, and, finally, the botched execution on Saturday, 10 January.

9. Only two, according to the *Chron. Pasch.*, p. 621, three according to Malalas 18.71 (p. 475).

10. Procopius puts the dismissal of the senators on the fifth day of the riot, i.e., Saturday; whereas the *Chron. Pasch.* puts it the next day. Whitby and Whitby (1989), p. 121, n. 359, think that Justinian, who now had troops from Thrace to quell the riot, had resolved on a positive strategy and wanted the senators to use their personal guards to defend their homes and prevent them being used by the rioters. If so, it was an unrealistic strategy.

11. *Wars* 1.24.21.

12. *PLRE* II, s.v. "Hypatius 6." See also Greatrex (1996).

13. Cf. Gregory (1984), p. 155. Greatrex (1997) argues that Justinian's efforts to conciliate the mob until the morning of the last day of the riot made matters worse. However, he lacked the resources to enforce a tough policy. The troops that were available in the

city had failed to restore order: see Malalas 18.71 (p. 474) who reports two unsuccessful attacks on the mob on the second day (Wednesday, 14 January) of the riot. Theophanes A.M. 6024 reports heavy casualties among the troops. The situation deteriorated to the extent that even the palace guard refused to obey orders: Procopius, *Wars* 1.24.45.

14. Procopius, *Wars* 1.24.26–39.

15. *PLRE* IIIB, s.v. "Origenes."

16. For the maxim, which was said to Dionysius I, tyrant of Syracuse in the fourth century B.C., see Isocrates, *Archidamus*, 45; Diodorus 14.8.5. See also Evans (1972), p. 33; Evans (1984).

17. Marcellinus, *anno* 532.

18. Rubin (1960), p. 109.

19. John Lydus (*De Mag.* 3.70.1) agrees; he gives a vivid picture of the taxpayers groaning under their burdens.

20. 9.14. John Lydus (*De Mag.* 3.70.5), who was in Constantinople, estimates almost 50,000 victims.

21. *Anth. Gr.* 7.592 (a funerary epigram for Hypatius); Procopius, *Wars* 1.24.58.

Chapter 5. Theodora's Friends and Enemies

1. *Nov.* 14.1 (p. 535).

2. *Anek.* 16.11.

3. *Anek.* 26.7–11; Malalas 18.43 (p. 449), who dates Priscus' exile to 529; Theophanes A.M. 6026 (A.D. 533–34), who reports that Justinian had Priscus made a deacon.

4. *PLRE* II, s.v. "Germanus 4"; cf. also Lemerle (1954), p. 283.

5. *Anek.* 5.8–15.

6. John of Ephesus, *Third Part of the Ecclesiastical History*, 1.32.

7. *Anek.* 5.32–33.

8. *CodJust.* 5.4.23.

9. Procopius, *Wars* 3.13.24; 6.4.6; 6.7.4.

10. *LibPont.*, s.v. "Silverius."

11. Possibly the mosaic of Theodora and her attendants in San Vitale (Ravenna) commemorates this betrothal. Antonina may be the woman on Theodora's left, and the young girl on Antonina's left would be Joaninna.

12. *Anek.* 4.1–12.

13. *Anek.* 4.37; 5.22.

14. *Anek.* 3.14. Procopius does not report how the secret was revealed.

15. *Wars* 3.10.7–21; *Anek.* 17.38; cf. *PLRE* IIIA, s.v. "Fl. Ioannes 11."

16. John Lydus, *De Mag.* 3.69.2–3.

17. Procopius, *Wars* 1.25.12–44; *Anek.* 2.16; 17.38–45, cf. Pazdernik (1994), pp. 268–70. The evidence of Lydus and Procopius is not necessarily contradictory.

18. *Anek.* 22; cf. *PLRE* IIIB, s.v. "Petrus *qui et* Barsymes 9"; cf. Treadgold (1997), p. 199.

19. *Nov.* 8.1.

20. *Anek.* 22.37–38; cf. Bellinger (1966), pp. 62–63, 72, 133–34.
21. *Anek.* 25.14–26.
22. *Anek.* 15.4.

Chapter 6. Theodora and Foreign Policy

1. Ps.-Dionysius of Tel-Mahre Pt. III, pp. 79–109; Witakowski (1996), pp. 74–98.
2. Procopius, *Wars* 2.23.6–11.
3. Bury (1958) II, p. 371. For the self-immolation of the Montanists, see *Anek.* 11.23.
4. *Wars* 2.8.30–35.
5. *Anek.* 2.32–35.
6. There is no good reason to think that it did. Justin II's wife, Sophia, who was Theodora's niece, wrote Khusru a letter appealing for a respite from war after the fall of Dara and Justin's lapse into madness. Khusru accepted her appeal.
7. Quoted, with some alterations, from R. Payne Smith, trans., *The Third Part of the Ecclesiastical History of John, Bishop of Ephesus* (Oxford, 1860), p. 252; cf. Michael the Syrian, 9.31.
8. Evans (1996a), p. 250; Frend (1975); Bury (1958), II, pp. 328–30; *CE*, s.v. "Nubia, Evangelization of," (William Y. Adams).
9. Thus Justin supported the mission of Kardutsat, bishop of Caucasian Albania, to the Sabir Huns even though Kardutsat was a Monophysite and he also cooperated with the Ethiopian king Elesboas, a Monophysite, against Dhu-Nuwas, the Jewish tyrant of Himyar (Yemen).
10. *Anek.* 16.1–5; 24.23.
11. 5.3.10–16; 4.12–31.
12. Cassiodorus, *Variae* 10.20, 10.21, trans., S. J. B. Barnish.
13. *Anek.* 11.16–20.

Chapter 7. The Theological Dilemma

1. The label "Diphysite" is used during this period whereas "Monophysite" is not, and hence it is somewhat anachronistic to speak of "Monophysites" in the reign of Justinian. However, like most historians of the period, I use the term for the sake of convenience.
2. Vasiliev (1950), p. 146–78.
3. Ps.-Dionysius of Tel-Mahre, p. 16 = Witakowski (1996), p. 18. The diptychs were lists of names and church councils, sometimes inscribed on double tablets of ivory, which were read out by the deacon during the Eucharist.
4. The *Tomus ad Flavianum* was a letter that Pope Leo the Great sent before the second Council of Ephesus to Flavian, the patriarch of Antioch, in which he set forth the Diphysite position, perhaps more baldly than he intended. It was not debated at Ephesus, but it formed the basis for the Chalcedonian Creed.
5. The *Trisagion* repeats three times the petition "Holy God, Holy Mighty One,

Holy Immortal One, have mercy upon us." Between 468 and 470, the patriarch of Antioch, Peter the Fuller, added, "Who was crucified for us" after "Holy Immortal One." For Peter, patriarch (469?–74; 476–77; 482–88) see *ODB*, s.v. "Peter the Fuller." Peter accepted the *Henotikon* in 482 before he was reappointed to his see.

6. Malalas 16.19 (pp. 407–8).

7. Capizzi (1994), pp. 53–54.

8. Michael the Syrian, 9.24. Michael's account is garbled, but if there is any truth to it, it would be our earliest instance of Theodora acting on behalf of the Monophysites.

9. John of Ephesus, *Lives* xiii (PO 17, pp. 187–94); Ps.-Dionysius of Tel-Mahre (Witakowski 1996, pp. 31–32); cf. Allen (1980), p. 472.

10. Garland (1999), p. 25. The adjoining palace church of Saints Peter and Paul seems to have been a favorite of Latin-speaking Chalcedonians in Constantinople.

11. *CodJust.* 1.5.

12. Harvey (1990), pp. 101–3. See also Duchesne (1915), passim.

13. John of Ephesus, *Life of John, Bishop of Thella*, PO 18; also Elias, *Vita Iohannis,* CSCO 8 (Script. Syri); cf. Frend (1972), pp. 260–62.

14. Zachariah of Mitylene, 9.15. Trans. F. J. Hamilton and E. W. Brooks.

15. *Vita Sabae* 71. Mar Saba returned to Palestine and died in his Lavra there on 5 December 532, at the age of about ninety-four. His motive for coming to Constantinople was not merely to lend support to the Chalcedonians but also to warn Justinian of the spread of Origenism in the Palestinian monasteries (see below, pp. 00). In Rome, a church dedicated to San Saba was built on the Aventine Hill by Palestinian monks fleeing from the East in the seventh century, and though the original does not survive, there is still a church of San Saba on the site: Alta MacAdam, *Rome and Environs* (Blue Guide) (London, 1989), p. 235.

16. Elias, *Vita*, p. 60, mentions their efforts to win his favor with gifts.

17. Vasiliev (1950), pp. 106–7.

18. Cassiodorus, *Variae* 9.15, from Athalaric to John II, dated to 533, is short of details but alludes clearly to a contested election as well as simony.

19. *CodJust.* 1.1.6; *Chron. Pasch. anno* 533 (p. 630), cf. *LibPont.*, s.v. "John II."

20. Zachariah of Mitylene, 9.16; Cf. Frend (1972), pp. 264–65; Frend (1973), pp. 2–24.

21. Cf. Capizzi (1994), p. 64.

22. PO 18, p. 678.

23. John of Ephesus, *Lives* ii (PO 17, pp. 18–35); Michael the Syrian, p. 22; Diehl (1904), pp. 81–83; Harvey (1990), pp. 84–86.

24. There is an interesting theological point here. At this time, the shift to infant baptism was already taking place, but people of the theater were beyond the pale. Theodora may not yet have been baptized, though it is more probable that her baptism by Z'ura was a second baptism, her first having been administered by a Chalcedonian, for the coronation ceremonies involved taking the Eucharist from a Chalcedonian patriarch. By accepting baptism from Z'ura, Theodora was taking a step toward recognizing a Monophysite priesthood.

25. Cf. Frend (1976), p. 77: "The touchstone of Severus' religious outlook was 'accu-

racy' of doctrine which involved the acceptance, as he says, of every word of Cyril of Alexandria as canonical, and the toleration of the *Henotikon* only in the sense that it annulled the definition of Chalcedon."

26. Ps.-Zachariah of Mitylene, 9.15.

27. Amalasuintha's murder should probably be dated about the end of April: see Bury, *LRE* II, p. 164, n. 3.

28. *Variae* 10.20.3.

29. See Victor Tonn., *anno* 540.

30. Cf. Ps.-Zachariah of Mytilene, 9.19.

31. *LibPont.*, s.v. "Agapitus"; Malalas 18.83 (p. 479); Theophanes A.M. *Chron.* 6029 (A.D. 536/7); cf. Diehl (1904), pp. 253–67; Evans (1996a), pp. 183–84; Bridge (1978), pp. 129–31.

32. CSCO 2, pp. 358–62.

33. Duchesne (1915), p. 71.

34. John of Ephesus, *Lives of the Eastern Saints:* PO 17.i: "The Five Blessed Patriarchs."

35. CSCO 2, pp. 351–57.

36. PO I, pp. 459–60.

37. *CE*, s.v. "Gaianus"; "Theodosius I" (E. R. Hardy), cf. John of Nikiu, chap. 92.

38. Capizzi (1994), pp. 66–68.

Chapter 8. Theodora's Quest for a New Strategy

1. Zachariah of Mytilene 9.19; John of Ephesus, PO 17, pp. 18–35; *LibPont.*, s.v. "Agapitus." See also *DHP,* s.v. "Agapet Ier ou Agapit" (Christiane Fraisse-Coué).

2. *Nov.* 42, trans. (with some modifications) from Ure (1951), pp. 124–26.

3. The Councils of Nicaea, Constantinople, Ephesus, and Chalcedon.

4. John of Ephesus, PO 18, p. 525.

5. Severus of Ashmounein, PO I, p. 466; cf. Frend (1972), pp. 274–76.

6. *Anek.* 27.11–19.

7. *PLRE* II, s.v. "Arsenius 3."

8. Capizzi (1994), p. 74; cf. *DHP,* s.v. "Silvère" (Christiane Fraisse-Coté).

9. Victor Tunn., *anno* 542, reports that Theodora had a written promise from Vigilius and that Antonina forced Vigilius to write to the Monophysites Theodosius, Severus, and Anthimus to say that he was in agreement with them.

10. *PLRE* IIIB, s.v. "Narses I."

11. *PLRE* II, s.v. "Reparatus I."

12. Lemerle (1954), pp. 285–86.

13. Michael the Syrian, 9.25.

14. 3.69.

15. *Wars* 2.10.4–5.

16. Cf. Treadgold (1997), pp. 197–98. Treadgold dates Harith's request to fall 542, noting that "Justinian was still gravely ill" from the plague.

17. John of Ephesus, *Life* of James: PO 17, pp. 690-97; cf. Frend (1972), pp. 285-87, also R. Butin, *CathEnc.*, s.v. "Baradaeus."

18. *Anek.* 4.1-13.

19. *Wars* 2.22.9-11.

20. *Anek.* 12.24-26.

21. Capizzi (1994), pp. 85-92; Witakowski (1987), p. 48.

Chapter 9. The Coercion of Rome

1. Capizzi (1994), pp. 77-80. For Origen, see *ODB*, s.v. "Origen"; *Dict. de Spir.*, s.v. "Origène" (Henri Crouzel).

2. Gerostergios (1982), pp. 41-48; Capizzi (1994), pp. 80-85.

3. Liberatus, *Breviarium*, 24.

4. Capizzi (1994), pp. 99-131; Evans (1996a), pp. 187-90; *DHP*, s.v. "Vigile" (Claire Sotinel).

5. Cf. Fitton (1976), who suggests gangrene.

Chapter 10. Afterword

1. Procopius, *Wars* 7.30.3-4, 7.30.25. In fact, there was a truce with Persia at this time, but it did not cover Lazica, modern Georgia, where the war still went on, nor did it stop skirmishes between the Lakmid Saracens, Persia's allies, and the Ghassanids. See Evans (1996a), pp. 166-67.

2. *Wars* 7.35.9.

3. *In Laudem Justini Augusti Minoris* 2.265-66; cf. Evans (1996a), p. 261.

4. Garland (1999), p. 24, quotes a letter of Severus where he points out Theodora's failure to distinguish between *physis* (nature) and *prosopon* (person). Theodora's mistake was no doubt shared by most of the lay population and most of the monks as well.

5. *CathEnc.*, s.v. "Baradaeus, Jacob" (R. Butin). Cf. G. Krüger, *Hastings' Encyclopedia*, s.v. "Monophysitism."

6. *Life* of John, Bishop of Hephaestopolis: PO 18, p. 529.

7. John of Ephesus, "Concerning the Holy Communities which Theodora the Queen gathered together at Constantinople": PO 18, p. 679.

8. 9.21.

9. Quoted by Debidour (1877), p. 51.

10. *Nov.* 8.1.

11. Quoted from *Late Antiquity*, s.v. "Theodora."

12. *Anek.* 14.8.

13. *Nov.* 117.15.

14. *Nov.* 134.10.

15. Diehl (1904), pp. 217-30; Evans (1996a), pp. 209-10; Fisher (1978), pp. 256-58; Cantarella (1987), pp. 139, 164.

16. Evans (1996a), pp. 255-56.

17. Mango (1972b), pp. 104–5.

18. The lives of the emperors and some of their empresses are available on the Web page, *De Imperatoribus Romanis.* On Domnica Augusta, see Thomas Banchich's brief essay.

19. *De Regno* 14. See in general Holum (1982), pp. 48–77.

20. Evans (1996a), p. 155.

21. Cf. Treadgold (1997), p. 225.

22. See Lynda Garland's essays on Sophia and Ino on the *De Imperatoribus Romanis* Web page.

Bibliography

Primary Sources

Anekdota - Procopius, *The Anecdota or Secret History*. Text and translation by H. B. Dewing. *LCL*. London/Cambridge, Mass. 1935.

Choricius of Gaza - Choricii Gazaei *Opera*. Ed. Richard Foerster. 1929, repr. Stuttgart, 1972.

Chron. Pasch. - *Chronicon Paschale 284–628 A.D.* Trans. with introduction by Michael Whitby and Mary Whitby. Liverpool, 1989.

Coleman-Norton (1966) - Coleman-Norton, P. R., *Roman State and Christian Church. A Collection of Legal Documents to A.D. 535*. London, 1966.

History of the Patriarchs of Alexandria - History of the Patriarchs of the Coptic Church of Alexandria by Severus of Ashmounein, trans. from the Arabic by B. Evetts, II: Peter I (300–11) to Benjamin I (622–61), (*PO* I).

John of Ephesus, *HistEccl. Pars Tertia* - *Historiae Ecclesiasticae Pars Tertia*, ed. E. W. Brooks, 2 vols. (Paris, 1936, repr. Louvain 1952) with Latin translation. English translation: R. Payne Smith, trans. and editor, *The Third Part of the Ecclesiastical History of John of Ephesus*. Oxford, 1860.

Corippus, *Laud.* - Flavius Cresconius Corippus, *In laudem Iustini Augusti Minoris*, ed. Av. Cameron (London, 1976), with English translation.

John of Ephesus, *Lives* - *Lives of the Eastern Saints*, ed. E. W. Brooks. *PO* 17 (1923), 1–307; *PO* 18 (1924), 513–698; *PO* 18 (1926), 153–285.

Vita Iohannis - *Vita Iohannis Episcopi Tellae auctore Elia*, trans. into Latin by E. W. Brooks. CSCO 8 (*Scriptores Syri*), pp. 20–69.

Vita Sabae - Cyril of Scythopolis, *Vie de S. Sabas* in A.-J. Festugière, *Les moines d'Orient*, vol. 3. Paris, 1962–63.

LibPont. - *The Book of the Pontiffs* (*Liber Pontificalis*). *The Ancient Biographies of the First Ninety Roman Bishops to A.D. 715*. Trans. with introduction by Raymond Davis. Translated Texts for Historians, Latin Series V. Liverpool, 1989.

Malalas - *The Chronicle of John Malalas*. Trans. and commentary by Elizabeth Jeffreys, Michael Jeffreys, and Roger Scott. *Byzantina Australiensia* 4. Melbourne, 1986.

Marcellinus - *The Chronicle of Marcellinus*. Latin text (Mommsen ed.), trans. and commentary by Brian Croke. *Byzantina Australiensia* 7. Sydney, 1995.

Michael the Syrian - *Chronique de Michel le Syrien,* trans. and ed. J.-B. Chabot, 4 vols. Paris, 1899–24, repr. Brussels 1960.

Patria - *Patria Konstantinoupoleos* in *Scriptores originum Constantinopolitanarum,* ed. Th. Preger. Leipzig, 1907.

Procopius, *Wars* - Procopius, *History of the Wars,* trans. H. B. Dewing. *LCL.* 6 vols. London/New York, 1914–28.

Pseudo-Dionysius of Tel-Mahre - *Chronicle, Pt. III* of Pseudo-Dionysius of Tel-Mahre, trans. with notes and introduction by Witold Witakowski. Liverpool, 1996.

Theophanes - *Chronographia,* ed. C. de Boor, 2 vols. Leipzig, 1883–85; repr. Hildesheim, 1963. Translated into English with introduction and commentary by Cyril Mango and Roger Scott, with the assistance of Geoffrey Greatrex: *The Chronicle of Theophanes the Confessor: Byzantine and Near Eastern History,* A.D. *284–813.* Oxford/New York, 1997.

Variae - The *Variae* of Magnus Aurelius Cassiodorus Senator, trans. with commentary and introduction by S. J. B. Barnish. Translated Texts for Historians XII, 1992.

Zach Myt - *The Syriac Chronicle* known as that of Zachariah of Mytilene. London, 1899.

Zonaras - Ioannis Zonarae *Epitome Historiarum,* ed. L. Dindorf. 5 vols. Leipzig, 1869–71.

Secondary Sources

Allen (1980) - Allen, Pauline, "Zachariah Scholasticus and the *Historia Ecclesiastica* of Evagrius Scholasticus," *Journal of Theological Studies* n.s. 31 (1980), pp. 471–88.

Bakker (1985) - Bakker, Gerard, "The Buildings at Alahan," in Mary Gough, ed., *Alahan: An Early Christian Monastery in Southern Turkey.* Pontifical Institute of Medieval Studies, LXXIII. Toronto, 1985, pp. 75–153.

Beck (1986) - Beck, Hans-George, *Kaiserin Theodora und Prokop. Der Historiker und sein Opfer.* Munich, 1986.

Bellinger (1966) - Bellinger, Alfred R., *Catalogue of the Byzantine Coins in the Dumbarton Oaks Collection and the Whitteman Collection.* I: *Anastasius I to Maurice.* Washington, D.C., 1966.

Boak (1919) - Boak, Arthur Edward Romilly, "Imperial Coronation Ceremonies in the Fifth and Sixth Centuries," *HSCP* 30 (1919), pp. 37–47.

Bridge (1978) - Bridge, Antony, *Theodora. Portrait in a Byzantine Landscape.* London, 1978.

Browning (1971) - Browning, Robert, *Justinian and Theodora.* London, 1971.

Bury (1897) - Bury, J. B., "The Nika Riot," *Journal of Hellenic Studies* 17 (1897), pp. 92–119.

Bury (1908) - Gibbon, Edward, *The History of the Decline and Fall of the Roman Empire,* ed. J. B. Bury. 3d ed., 1908.

Bury (1958) - Bury, J. B., *History of the Later Roman Empire from the Death of Theodosius I to the Death of Justinian*. Repr. New York, 1958.

Cameron (1974) - Cameron, Alan, "Heresies and Factions," *Byzantion* 44 (1974), pp. 92–120.

Cameron (1976) - Cameron, Alan, *Circus Factions. Blues and Greens at Rome and Byzantium*. Oxford, 1976.

Cameron (1978) - Cameron, Alan, "The House of Anastasius," *Greek, Roman and Byzantine Studies* 19 (1978), pp. 259–76.

Cameron, Av. (1981) - Cameron, Averil, "Images of Authority: Élites and Icons in Late Sixth-Century Byzantium," in Margaret Mullett and Roger Scott, eds., *Byzantium and the Classical Tradition* (University of Birmingham Spring Symposium of Byzantine Studies, 1979). Birmingham, 1981. Repr. from *Past and Present* 84 (1979), pp. 3–25.

Cameron, Av. (1985) - Cameron, Averil, *Procopius and the Sixth Century*. Berkeley/Los Angeles, 1985.

Cantarella (1987) - Cantarella, Eva, *Pandora's Daughters*. Baltimore, 1987.

Capizzi (1994) - Capizzi, Carmelo, *Giustiniano I tra politica e religione*. Messina, 1994.

Carney (1971) - Carney, T. F., *Bureaucracy in Traditional Society: Romano-Byzantine Buraucracies Viewed from Within*. Lawrence, Kan., 1971.

Chadwick (1967) - Chadwick, Henry, *The Early Church*. Harmondsworth, 1967.

Clark (1993) - Clark, Gillian, *Women in Late Antiquity. Pagan and Christian Lifestyles*. Oxford, 1993.

Cottas (1931) - Cottas, Vénétia, *Le théâtre à Byzance*. Paris, 1931.

Croke (1990) - Croke, Brian, "The Early Development of Byzantine Chronicles," *Studies in John Malalas (Byzantina Australiensia* 6). Sydney, 1990, pp. 27–38.

Daube (1967) - Daube, David, "The Marriage of Justinian and Theodora. Logical and Theological Reflections," *Catholic University of America Law Review* 16 (1967), pp. 380–99.

Dawes and Baynes (1948) - Dawes, Elizabeth and Baynes, Norman, *Three Byzantine Saints*. Oxford, 1948, repr. Crestwood, N.Y., 1977.

Debidour (1877) - Debidour, A., *De Theodora Justiniani Augusti Uxore*. Thesis, Université de Paris, 1877.

Diehl (1901) - Diehl, Charles, *Justinien et la Civilisation Byzantine au VIe siècle*. Paris, 1901.

Diehl (1904) - Diehl, Charles, *Théodora, impératrice de Byzance*. Paris, 1904.

Downey (1968) - Downey, Glanville, *Justinian and the Imperial Office: Lectures in Memory of Louise Taft Semple*. Cincinnati, 1968.

Duchesne (1915) - Duchesne, L., "Les Protégés de Théodora," *Mélanges d'archéologie et d'histoire de l'école française de Rome* 35 (1915), pp. 57–79.

Evans (1972) - Evans, J. A. S., *Procopius*. New York, 1972.

Evans (1984) - Evans, J. A. S., "The 'Nika' Rebellion and the Empress Theodora," *Byzantion* 54 (1984), pp. 380–82.

Evans (1996a) - Evans, J. A. S., *The Age of Justinian: The Circumstances of Imperial Power*. London, 1996.

Evans (1996b) - Evans, J. A. S., "The Dates of Procopius' Works: A Recapitulation of the Evidence," *Greek, Roman and Byzantine Studies* 37 (1996), pp. 301-13.

Evans (1996c) - Evans, J. A. S., "The Monophysite Persecution: The Eastern View," *Ancient World* 27/2 (1996), pp. 191-96.

Evans (1999) - Evans, James Allan, "The Flavour of Anatolia," *Contemporary Review* 275 (1999), pp. 113-68.

Every (1979) - Every, George, "Was Vigilius a Victim or an Ally of Justinian?" *Heythrop Journal* 20 (1979), pp. 257-66.

Fisher (1978) - Fisher, Elizabeth A., "Theodora and Antonina in the *Historia Arcana*: Fact and/or Fiction?" *Arethusa* 11 (1978), pp. 253-79.

Fitton (1976) - Fitton, James, "The Death of Theodora," *Byzantion* 46 (1976), p. 119.

Forsyth (1968) - Forsyth, George H., "The Monastery of St. Catherine at Mount Sinai. The Church and Fortress of Justinian," *DOP* 22 (1968), pp. 1-19.

Fowden (1999) - Elizabeth Key Fowden, *The Barbarian Plain. Saint Sergius between Rome and Iran*. Berkeley, 1999.

Frend (1972) - Frend, W. H. C., *The Rise of the Monophysite Movement: Chapters in the History of the Church in the Fifth and Sixth Centuries*. Cambridge, 1972.

Frend (1973) - Frend, W. H. C., "Old and New Rome in the Age of Justinian," in Derek Baker, ed., *Relations between East and West in the Middle Ages*. Edinburgh, 1973.

Frend (1975) - Frend, W. H. C., "The Mission to Nubia: an Episode in the Struggle for Power in Sixth-Century Byzantium," *Travaux du Centre d'archéologie méditerranéen de l'Academie Polonaise des Sciences, t. 16. Études de Travaux* VIII, pp. 10-16, repr. *Town and Country in the Early Christian Centuries*. Variorum, London, 1980.

Frend (1976) - Frend, W. H. C., "Eastern Attitudes to Rome during the Acacian Schism," *Studies in Church History* 13 (ed. D. Baker), pp. 69-81.

Frend (1980) - Frend, W. H. C., "The Monophysites and the Transition between the Ancient World and the Middle Ages," *Atti dei Convegni Lincei 45: Convegno internazionale "Passagio dal mondo antico al Medio Evo da Teodosio a San Gregorio Magno" (Roma, 25-28 maggio 1977)*. Rome; Accademia Nazionale dei Lincei, 1980, repr. *Archaeology and History in the Study of Early Christianity*. Variorum, London, 1988.

Garland (1999) - Garland, Lynda, *Byzantine Empresses: Women and Power in Byzantium, A.D. 527-1204*. London/New York, 1999; s.v. "Theodora, Wife of Justinian (527-48)," pp. 11-39.

Geanakoplos (1966) - Geanakoplos, Deno John, "Church Building and 'Caesaropapism,'" *Greek, Roman and Byzantine Studies* 7 (1966), pp. 167-86.

Gerostorgios (1982) - Gerostorgios, Asterios, *Justinian the Great: The Emperor and Saint*. Belmont, Mass., 1982.

Greatrex (1996) - Greatrex, Geoffrey, "Flavius Hypatius, *quem vidit validum Parthus sensitque timendum*," *Byzantion* 66 (1996), pp. 120–42.

Greatrex (1997) - Greatrex, Geoffrey, "The Nika Riot: A Reappraisal," *Journal of Hellenic Studies* 117 (1997), pp. 60–86.

Greatrex (1998) - Greatrex, Geoffrey, *Rome and Persia at War, 502–532*. Leeds, 1998.

Gregory (1984) - Gregory, Timothy E., "Urban Violence in Late Antiquity," in R. Marchese, ed., *Aspects of Greco-Roman Urbanism*, pp. 138–61. BAR 188. Oxford, 1984.

Hardy (1968) - Hardy, Edward R., "The Egyptian Policy of Justinian," *Dumbarton Oaks Papers* 22 (1968), pp. 21–41.

Harrison (1986) - Harrison, R. M., *Excavations at Saraçhane in Istanbul, I. The Excavations, Structure and Architectural Decoration, Small Finds, Coins, Bones and Molluscs*. Dumbarton Oaks Research Library and Collection, Princeton, 1986.

Harvey (1990) - Harvey, Susan Ashbrook, *Asceticism and Society in Crisis: John of Ephesus and "The Lives of the Eastern Saints."* Berkeley, 1990.

Henry (1967) - Henry, Patrick, "A Mirror for Justinian: The *Ekthesis* of Agapetus Diaconus," *Greek, Roman and Byzantine Studies* 8 (1967), 281–308.

Hill (1940) - Hill, Sir George, *A History of Cyprus I: To the Conquest by Richard Lion Heart*. Cambridge, 1940.

Holmes (1912) - Holmes, William Gordon, *The Age of Justinian and Theodora*. 2d ed. I–II. London, 1912.

Holum (1982) - Holum, Kenneth G., *Theodosian Empresses: Women and Imperial Domination in Late Antiquity*. Berkeley, 1982.

Houssaye (1885) - Houssaye, Henri, "L'impératrice Théodora," *Revue des deux mondes* 67 (1885), pp. 568–97.

Janin (1964) - Janin, R., *Constantinople Byzantine. Développement urbain et répertoire topographique*. 2d ed., Paris, 1964.

Karagiannopoulos (1995) - Karagiannopoulos, Ioannes E., *Historia Vizantinou Kratous*. I: *Historia Proinou Vizantines Peridou*. Thessaloniki, 1995.

Karlin-Hayter (1973) - Karlin-Hayter, Patricia, "Les *Akta dia Kalopodion*. Le contexte réligieux et politique," *Byzantion* 43 (1973), pp. 84–107.

Krautheimer (1965) - Krautheimer, Richard, *Early Christian and Byzantine Architecture*. Harmondsworth, 1965.

Lemerle (1954) - Lemerle, Paul, "Invasions et migrations dans les Balkans depuis la fin de l'époque romaine jusqu'à VIIIe siècle," *Revue historique* 211 (1954), pp. 265–308.

Lemerle (1964) - Lemerle, Paul, *A History of Byzantium*. New York, 1964.

Mango (1972a) - Mango, Cyril, *The Arts of the Byzantine Empire, 312–1453*. Englewood Cliffs, N.J., 1972.

Mango (1972b) - Mango, Cyril, "The Church of Saints Sergius and Bacchus at Constantinople and the Alleged Tradition of Octagonal Palatine Churches," *JÖB* 21 (1972), pp. 189–93.

Mango and Scott (1997) - *The Chronicle of Theophanes the Confessor: Byzantine and*

Near Eastern History, A.D. 284–813. Translated into English with introduction and commentary by Cyril Mango and Roger Scott, with the assistance of Geoffrey Greatrex. Oxford/New York, 1997.

Matthews (1971) - Matthews, Thomas F., *The Early Churches of Constantinople: Architecture and Liturgy.* University Park, Pa./London, 1971.

Moorhead (1994) - Moorhead, John, *Justinian.* London/New York, 1994.

Norwich (1990) - John Julius Norwich, *Byzantium, the Early Centuries.* New York, 1988, repr. London, 1990.

Pazdernik (1994) - Pazdernik, Charles, "'Our Most Pious Consort Given Us by God': Dissident Reactions to the Partnership of Justinian and Theodora, A.D. 525–548," *Classical Antiquity* 13 (1994), pp. 256–81.

Rice (1954) - Rice, David Talbot, *Byzantine Art,* 2d ed., Harmondsworth, 1965, repr. with revisions, 1962.

Rubin (1960) - Rubin, Berthold, *Das Zeitalter Iustinians. I.* Berlin, 1960.

Scott (1990) - Scott, Roger, "The Byzantine Chronicle after Malalas," *Studies in John Malalas (Byzantina Australiensia* 6). Sydney, 1990, pp. 38–54.

Stein (1949) - Stein, Ernst, *Histoire du Bas-Empire II.* Paris/Brussels/Amsterdam, 1949.

Storrs and O'Brien (1930) - Storrs, Sir Ronald, and O'Brien, Bryan Justin, *A Handbook of Cyprus.* London, 1930.

Traversari (1960) - Traversari, Gaetano, *Gli spettacoli in acqua nel teatro-tardo-antico.* Rome, 1960.

Treadgold (1997) - Treadgold, Warren, *A History of the Byzantine State and Society.* Stanford, Calif., 1997.

Ure (1951) - Ure, Percy Neville, *Justinian and His Age.* Harmondsworth, 1951.

Vasiliev (1950) - Vasiliev, A. A., *Justin the First: An Introduction to the Epoch of Justinian the Great.* Cambridge, Mass., 1950.

Whitby and Whitby (1989) - *Chronicon Paschale 284–628 A.D.* Translated with notes and introduction by Michael Whitby and Mary Whitby. Liverpool, 1989.

Witakowski (1987) - Witakowski, Witold, *The Syriac Chronicle of Pseudo-Dionysius of Tel-Mahre: A Study in the History of Historiography.* Uppsala, 1987.

Witakowski (1996) - *Chronicle.* Known also as the *Chronicle of Zuqnin: pt. III, Pseudo-Dionysius of Tel-Mahre.* Translated with notes and introduction by Witold Witakowski. Liverpool, 1996.

Index

Printed and bound by CPI Group (UK) Ltd, Croydon, CR0 4YY

27/03/2025

14649109-0001